my **revision** notes

CW00972447

Edexcel B GCSE GEOGRAPHY

UNIT 1: DYNAMIC PLANET

Nigel Yates

HODDER EDUCATION
AN HACHETTE UK COMPANY

In order to ensure that this resource offers high quality support for the associated Edexcel qualification, it has been through a review process by the awarding organisation to confirm that it fully covers the teaching and learning content of the specification or part of a specification at which it is aimed, and demonstrates an appropriate balance between the development of subject skills, knowledge and understanding, in addition to preparation for assessment.

While the publishers have made every attempt to ensure that advice on the qualification and its assessment is accurate, the official specification and associated assessment guidance materials are the only authoritative source of information and should always be referred to for definitive guidance.

No material from an endorsed resource will be used verbatim in any assessment set by Edexcel.

Endorsement of a resource does not mean that the resource is required to achieve this Edexcel qualification, nor does it mean that it is the only suitable material available to support the qualification, and any resource lists produced by the awarding organisation shall include this and other appropriate resources.

The Publishers would like to thank the following for permission to reproduce copyright material:

Photo credits: p.11 © EPA/Geraldo Caso; p.16 Visit Greenland /http://www.flickr.com/photos/ilovegreenland/6034619859/http://creativecommons.org/licenses/by/2.0/deed.en_GB; p.42 (left) © Getty Images/Robert Harding World Imagery, (right) © Eye Ubiquitous/Alamy; p.54 © Jim Steinberg/Science Photo Library; p.55 Suzanne Knights/public domain/http://en.wikipedia.org/wiki/File:Interlocking_spurs,_Ashes_Hollow.jpg; p.56 © Jens Hilberger – Fotolia; p.79 © Steve Morgan / Alamy.

Acknowledgements: Page 28 From a joint report by the International Programme on the State of the Ocean (IPSO) and the International Union for Conservation of Nature (IUCN) presented to the United Nations, June 2011; Figure 7 on page 20 is adapted from the graph 'Projected changes in global temperature' from GRID-Arendal reproduced at http://www.grida.no/publications/vg/climate/page/3076.aspx; Figure 1 on page 23 is based on an original artwork in *Biology 6th Edition*, by Sylvia S Mader, published by McGraw Hill Inc. (1996); Figure 4 on page 35 is adapted from a map created by the Centre for Environmental Systems Research, University of Kassel, Germany; Figure 5 on page 36 is adapted from the map 'Access to safe drinking water' from GRID-Arendal reproduced at http://www.grida.no/graphicslib/detail/access-to-safe-drinking-water_de64, originally drawn by Hugo Ahlenius, UNEP/GRID-Arendal; Figure 2 on page 52 is based on an artwork by David Rees-Jones; Figure 1 on page 62 is adapted from the map 'Coral reefs of the world classified by threat from global activities' from the report *Reefs at Risk Revisited* published by the World Resources Institute http://pdf.wri.org/reefs_at_risk_revisited.pdf; Figure 4 on page 70 is adapted from the map 'Marine protected areas in coral reef regions classified according to management effectiveness rating' from the report *Reefs at Risk Revisited* published by the World Resources Institute http://pdf.wri.org/reefs_at_risk_revisited.pdf; Figure 1 on page 77 is based on a group of maps 'The Disappearance of Lake Chad in Africa' from GRID-Arendal reproduced at http://www.grida.no/publications/vg/africa/page/3115.aspx.

Every effort has been made to trace all copyright holders, but if any have been inadvertently overlooked the Publishers will be pleased to make the necessary arrangements at the first opportunity.

Although every effort has been made to ensure that website addresses are correct at time of going to press, Hodder Education cannot be held responsible for the content of any website mentioned in this book. It is sometimes possible to find a relocated web page by typing in the address of the home page for a website in the URL window of your browser.

Hachette UK's policy is to use papers that are natural, renewable and recyclable products and made from wood grown in sustainable forests. The logging and manufacturing processes are expected to conform to the environmental regulations of the country of origin.

Orders:

please contact Bookpoint Ltd, 130 Milton Park, Abingdon, Oxon OX14 4SB.

Telephone: (44) 01235 827827.

Fax: (44) 01235 400401.

Lines are open 9.00 – 5.00, Monday to Saturday, with a 24-hour message answering service. Visit our website at www.hoddereducation.co.uk.

First published in 2012 by

Hodder Education,

An Hachette UK Company

338 Euston Road

London NW1 3BH

Impression number 5 4 3 2

Year 2016 2015 2014 2013

Cover photo © adimas/Fotolia.com

Illustrations by Barking Dog Art Design & Illustration

Typeset in Stempel Schneidler Std 11 points by Datapage (India) Pvt. Ltd.

Printed in Spain

A catalogue record for this title is available from the British Library

ISBN: 978 1444 164 473

Contents and revision planner

Unit 1 Dynamic Planet

Section A Dynamic Planet

Chapter 1 Restless Earth

How and why do Earth's tectonic plates move?

The Earth in cross-section

Revised

Figure 1 The Earth in cross-section

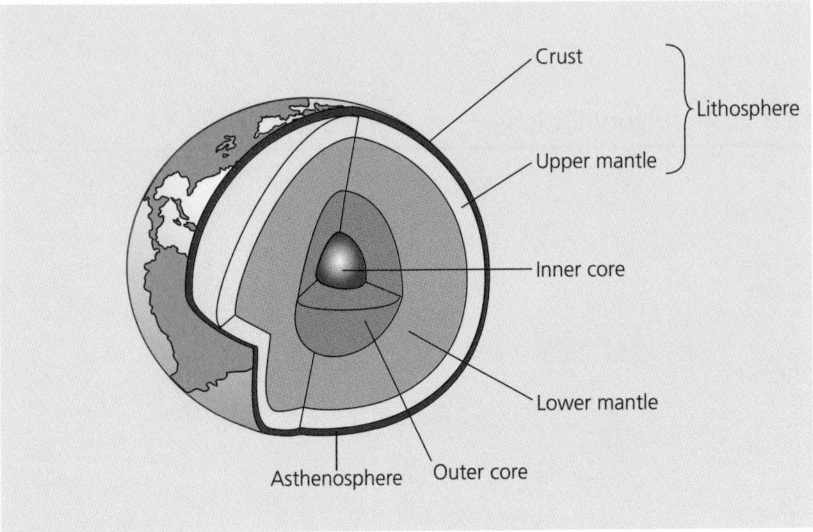

Layer		Physical state	Composition	Temperature (°C)
Lithosphere	**Continental crust**	Solid	Granite	Up to 900
	Oceanic crust	Solid	Basalt	Up to 900
	Upper mantle	Solid	Ultrabasic minerals	900–1000
Mantle	**Asthenosphere**	Partially molten	Peridotites	1000–1600
	Lower mantle	Solid	Silica-based minerals	1600–4000
Core	Outer core	Liquid: very dense	Iron/nickel	4000–5000
	Inner core	Solid: very dense	Iron/nickel	4000–5000

The Earth is made up of several different layers. The diameter of the Earth is about 13,000 km and the outer layer – the crust – is between 6 km and 60 km thick. So if we draw the Earth to scale with the diameter at 1.3 m the crust would be a very thin line indeed of between 0.6 mm and 6 mm. The upper mantle and the crust are known as the lithosphere.

Knowing the basics

There are three basic divisions – the **core**, the **mantle** and the **crust**. The crust is very thin compared with the other two. The core is intensely hot: 4000–5000 °C.

Stretch and challenge

There are many variations within each of the three layers, especially in the mantle. The very top of the mantle behaves like the crust.

The two types of crust

Revised

- Continental crust makes up most of the land area of the Earth. It is dominated by rocks that cool below the surface, such as granite. It is between 25 km and 80 km thick.
- Oceanic crust is much thinner – between 6 km and 8 km thick – and made up of rocks that cool on the surface, such as basalt.

How the Earth's tectonic plates move

Revised

Figure 2 Convection currents in the mantle

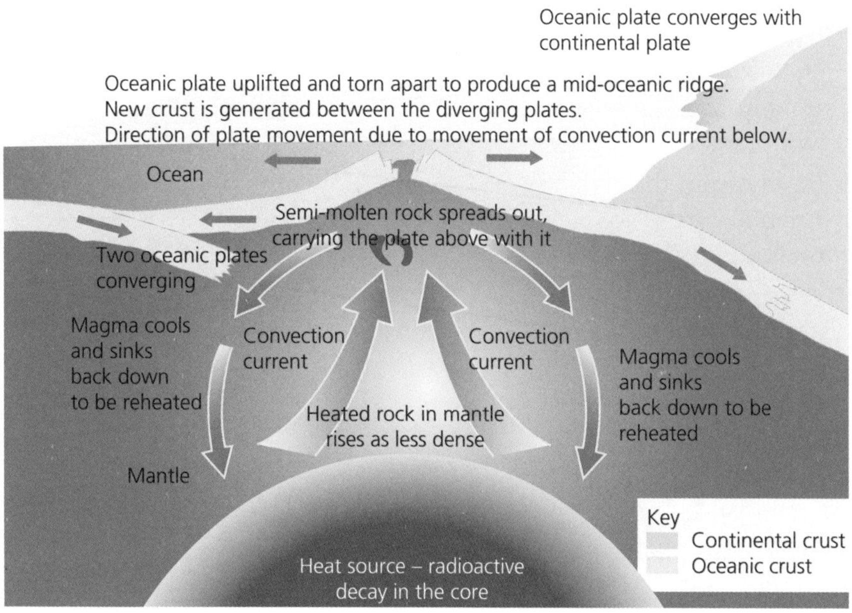

High temperatures in the core caused by gradual radioactive decay create rising limbs of material in the mantle, called **convection currents**. These cool and spread out as they rise before sinking again – just like a lava lamp! Some of this rising and falling material moves in sheets, creating movements in the crust above it, which is pulled apart to form new crust. In other places it rises as columns, creating **hotspots**.

The Earth has a **magnetic field** created by minerals, including iron, that rise and fall in the mantle. This field changes over time.

Stretch and challenge

Not all rising material creates movement – in some places the plates move over the hotspots.

exam tip

Make sure that you understand the command word. A question that asks you to *describe* how plates move is not the same as one that asks you to *explain* why they move.

Check your understanding

Tested

Place the following in the right order if you undertook a 'journey to the centre of the Earth': core, mantle, crust.

Different types of plate boundary

Revised

Knowing the basics

There are three main types of plate boundary:

- **constructive margins**
- **destructive margins**
- **conservative margins**.

Constructive margins

- It is thought that constructive margins are formed by rising magma splitting up continental crust and forming new oceans.
- The Eurasian plate is separating slowly from the North American plate. The mid-Atlantic ridge is a constructive margin sometimes visible above sea level, as in Iceland.
- This seems to be happening in East Africa today in its continental rift zone.

Destructive margins

- In some places, such as where the NAZCA plate meets the South American plate, oceanic plates collide with continental plates.
- When this occurs, the heavier basaltic oceanic lithosphere sinks beneath the continental plate.
- This process is known as **subduction** and creates a very deep ocean trench near the line of contact between the oceanic and continental plates.
- As an oceanic plate is subducted into the mantle it is subjected to increased pressure and temperature.
- These conditions cause some lightweight materials to melt and rise to the surface to form volcanoes.
- As a result, long chains of volcanoes, known as volcanic arcs, are located above subducted plates, usually above the location where the plate has reached a depth of about 100 km.
- The collision of the plates also lifts and buckles the continental plate, creating **fold mountains**; for example the Andes.

Figure 3 The main plates, margins and volcanoes

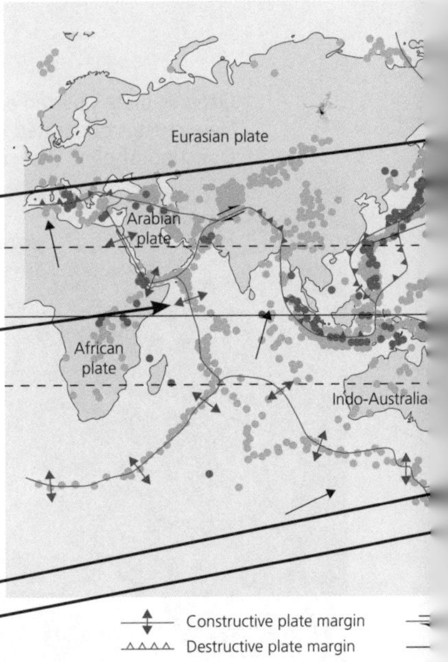

Figure 4 Margins and hotspots

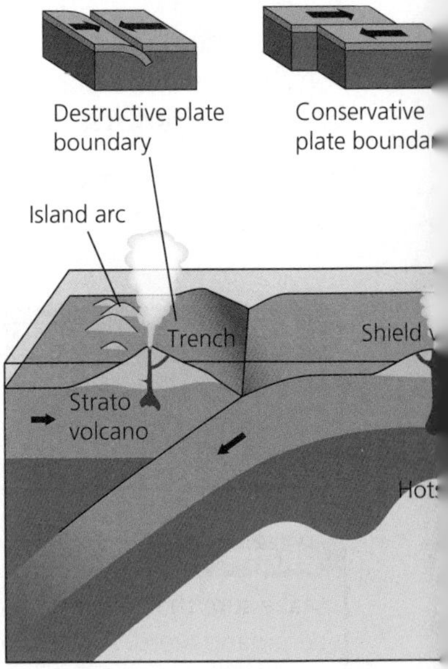

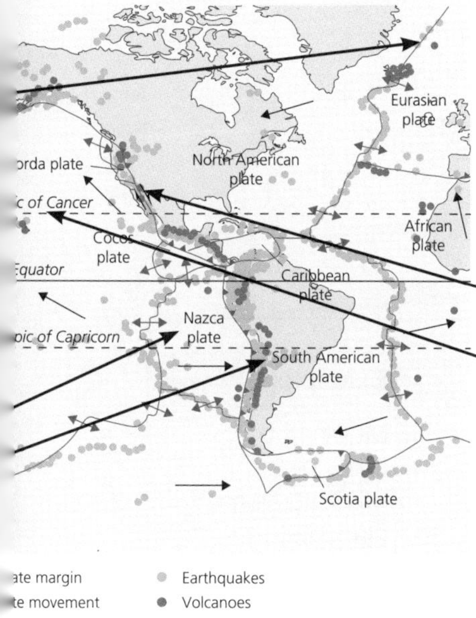

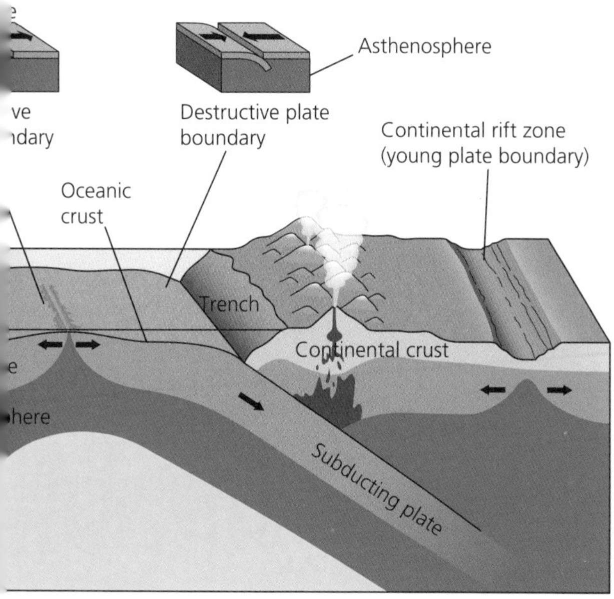

Conservative margins

Where plates slide past each other or move in the same direction but at different speeds then:

- no crust is formed or destroyed
- great strain builds up along the junction, with sudden lurches along the **fault**
- earthquakes are frequent and often large.

The best known example of this is the system of faults along the west coast of the USA, the best known of which is the San Andreas fault.

Knowing the basics

Hotspots are areas of rising plumes of magma in the asthenosphere which create volcanoes in the crust as it moves over them, leaving a long trail of islands or volcanoes.

Knowing the basics

New crust is made at constructive margins and old crust destroyed at destructive margins.

Stretch and challenge

Oceanic crust is created and destroyed. Continental crust is folded, crushed and compressed, but not destroyed.

exam tip

If you are asked to describe a pattern, start with a general point such as 'It is uneven ...'

Check your understanding

1 What are hotspots?

2 What is happening on constructive margins?

Tested

Different hazards and their causes

Revised

The impact of any **hazard**, including earthquakes and volcanoes, depends on:

- the size of the event
- the vulnerability of the population – how many people there are and how close they live
- the capacity of the population to cope – how prepared they are.

Different factors influence where volcanoes and earthquakes occur:

- Figure 3 shows that volcanoes are not evenly distributed. Because plate margins are essentially lines, so most volcanoes are found in lines.
- Where one finds volcanoes one also finds earthquakes, but earthquakes also occur on conservative margins and sometimes happen in regions many thousands of miles from plate margins.
- Not all volcanoes are found on plate margins. Some are found at hotspots where the crust is moving over a column of rising magma (e.g. in Hawaii).

There are also two main kinds of volcanic hazard: composite volcanoes and shield volcanoes. This table explains the differences between them. Composite volcanoes are much more dangerous to any human populations nearby.

Type	Form	Magma/lava type	Explosivity and frequency	Example(s)
Composite/ strato	Steep-sided Small area Alternate layers of ash and lava	Viscous/sticky – flows slowly Often 'freezes' in the central vent Made up of a mixture of basaltic and granitic material	Infrequent and sometimes unpredictable Pressure builds up over time	Mt Pinatubo (Philippines) Mt Sakurajima (Japan)
Shield	Gentle slopes (like a shield!) Large area Almost all lava	Fluid – flows quickly from many fissures Made up mostly of basalt	Very frequent and generally gentle eruptions	Mauna Loa (Hawaii, USA) Mt Nyiragongo (DRC)

Volcanic eruptions don't generally kill large numbers of people – at least not as a direct consequence of an eruption – because volcanoes are mountains and tend not to be located in areas where lots of people want to live. But many earthquake regions are very attractive areas to live and, despite the risks, some have high population densities. Earthquake events are less predictable and more dangerous than volcanoes.

What are the effects and management issues resulting from tectonic hazards?

The impact of earthquakes

Revised

A number of factors control the severity of earthquakes:

- the size of the movement
- the depth of the movement
- the type of material the shock wave passes through.

In general the impact of earthquakes varies according to:

- the strength of the event
- the distance from the **epicentre**
- the amount of warning
- the time of day
- the level of preparedness
- the quality of the emergency services.

For the most part the poorer the country is the greater the impact on people. On the other hand because the population in developed countries insure their property and businesses, the 'cost' of the disaster is often higher.

Knowing the basics

Remember that hazards don't necessarily lead to disasters. Much depends on how well prepared people are.

Stretch and challenge

Remember that the size of an event may be too great for even the most prepared countries. The death toll from the Japanese **tsunami** of 2011 reached over 18,000.

Whatever the impact it is helpful to split it into the following:

1 **Primary impacts** – the immediate effect of an earthquake on property and people. For earthquakes this is the people killed as a result of the shaking and property destruction.

2 **Secondary impacts** – the impact on property and people of an event after it has finished. Lack of shelter and basic supplies, as well as fires, are frequent secondary effects.

Check your understanding

Tested

Draw up a case study table for your chosen events.

Developed world example	**Earthquake event details**	**Disaster?**	**Future threats**
Name: Location:	When/how large:	Primary impacts on people/property: Secondary impacts:	
Developing world example	**Earthquake event details**	**Disaster?**	**Future threats**
Name: Location:	When/how large:	Primary impacts on people/property: Secondary impacts:	

exam tip

You may be asked for local details – two or three facts and figures about your case study will be enough.

Living with volcanoes

Revised

Volcanoes are **active**, **dormant** or **extinct**. Active volcanoes pose the greatest threat but dormant volcanoes can also be a danger:

- Mt St Helens was classified by some experts as 'dormant' before its famous 1980 eruption.
- In 2010, Iceland's Eyjafjallajökull volcano, one of the largest in the country, erupted for the first time in 200 years, disrupting air travel.

In and around Naples in southern Italy over 1 million people live within 9 km of Vesuvius, an active volcano best known for its AD79 eruption, which destroyed Pompeii and other Roman cities.

Knowing the basics

An extinct volcano cannot erupt but a dormant one can – it just hasn't for a very long time.

Knowing the basics

Volcanoes kill far more people with gas and ash than they do with lava.

As with earthquakes the impact of volcanoes can be separated into:

- **primary** – the initial effects of an eruption
- **secondary** – the longer-term impacts due to disruption of the economy and communications.

In the developed world higher incomes generally mean that the risks of secondary impacts are reduced.

Check your understanding

Tested

Draw up a case study table for your chosen events.

Developed world example	Eruption event details	Disaster?	Future threats
Name: Location:	When/how large:	Primary impacts on people/ property: Secondary impacts:	
Developing world example	**Eruption event details**	**Disaster?**	**Future threats**
Name: Location:	When/how large:	Primary impacts on people/ property: Secondary impacts:	

Prediction, warning and evacuation

Revised

Prediction of earthquakes and volcanoes is an uncertain business.

Preparedness – being ready	Mitigation – reducing the impact
Emergency plans in place	Hazard-resistant building design
Emergency services trained and funded	Disaster kits
Warning systems in place	Strengthening buildings
Evacuation plans	Planning/relocation
Training the population	

An example of mitigation is making buildings safer:

Developed world – make new buildings better	Developing world – make existing buildings better
New buildings more flexible, with a 'shear core'	Reduce the weight of the roofs
Foundations very deep but allow movement	Lightweight, hollow bricks used
Shock absorbers built into structure	Strengthen wall corners with wire mesh and cement
Cross bracing to prevent floors collapsing	Point external walls to prevent falling masonry

Knowing the basics

In the developed world more money is available to make new buildings safer. In the developing world it is important that existing buildings are made safer.

Stretch and challenge

Remember that in the fast growing cities of the developing world new buildings should also include the features often pioneered in the developed world.

exam tip

Remember that if you are asked to outline *one* method of improving buildings to help resist earthquakes then you should offer one point and a development of that point for the two marks available.

Figure 5 Earthquake damage in Chile, February 2010

Response and relief in Haiti – too little too late

Revised

The event

- It was the strongest earthquake in Haiti since 1770.
- The earthquake struck on 12 January 2010 at 4:53p.m.
- The 7.0 magnitude earthquake's epicentre was 10 miles west of Port-au-Prince and its 2 million inhabitants.
- The death count was estimated to be at least 220,000 and maybe as much as 350,000.
- At least 1.5 million people were made homeless.
- There were many aftershocks ranging in magnitude from 4.2 to 5.9.
- The earthquake was very similar to that which hit Christchurch in New Zealand in 2011 – this 7.1 magnitude earthquake destroyed 3000 buildings and killed 181 people.

The response

- Three million people were in need of emergency aid.
- The Red Cross dispatched a relief team from Geneva, and the UN's World Food Program flew in two planes with emergency food aid.
- World Vision, an **NGO**, provided food to 1.2 million people, emergency shelter for 41,000 families, delivered 16 million litres of clean water, installed 300 showers and 240 toilets in dozens of camps and were running health, education, child protection and livelihood programmes for tens of thousands of vulnerable children and affected adults.
- The Inter-American Development Bank immediately approved a $200,000 grant for emergency aid.
- President Obama promised $100 million in aid to Haiti on 14 January 2009. In comparison, one F-22 fighter bomber costs about $300 million.

The analysis

Haiti is a very poor country and remains so:

- Most of the help provided has been from private charities – from NGOs and not from governments.
- Women are especially badly affected and many are forced into prostitution.
- The country is still controlled by a tiny elite who may not get aid to the right people.

Check your understanding

Tested

Explain the difference between preparation and mitigation.

exam tip

If you are trying to introduce a new, second idea in your answer try to flag it up like this: 'Secondly, …'

Exam focus

1 Describe TWO characteristics of the mantle. [4]

2 Which of the following best describes the crust? [1]

A. A thin layer of basalt on the earth's surface.

B. A hot molten area of iron and nickel.

C. An area of solid material next to the core.

D. A solid layer that is made up of granitic and basaltic rocks.

3 What is a hotspot? [2]

4 Explain why tectonic plates move. [4]

5 Using Figure 3, describe the pattern of plate boundaries. [3]

6 Outline ONE process that takes place at a constructive margin. [2]

7 Outline how fold mountains are formed. [4]

8 Describe the process of subduction. [3]

9 Describe TWO characteristics of composite volcanoes. [4]

10 Explain why strato volcanoes are often very large with gentle sides. [2]

11 Outline the difference between primary and secondary impacts of an earthquake. [2]

12 For an earthquake that you have studied, outline TWO features of that event. [4]

13 Explain why evacuation in case of a volcanic eruption is expensive. [3]

14 Define the term 'dormant volcano'. [2]

15 Describe TWO ways of making buildings safer in the *developed* world. [4]

16 Describe TWO ways of making buildings safer in the *developing* world. [4]

Answers online Online

Chapter 2 Climate and Change

How and why has climate changed in the past?

Past climate change

Revised

The **weather** can change from minute to minute; in the UK it often does! **Climate** is best defined as the average weather conditions over a long period of time.

We know that climate has changed a great deal in the history of the Earth. This is shown by:

- fossils of animals and plants in regions they are not found in today
- evidence of glaciation in regions that are now free of ice
- evidence from rocks showing us the climate conditions when those rocks were formed
- evidence from ice cores in Greenland and Antarctica showing us how much carbon dioxide (CO_2) and oxygen was in the atmosphere when the ice was formed.

Figure 1 shows quite a regular pattern of highs and lows, almost like a cycle. This period, known as the **Quaternary**, was a period of rather colder temperatures for most of the time, leading to hugely expanded ice sheets covering much of Europe, Asia and North America.

Figure 1 Temperature change over the past 400,000 years

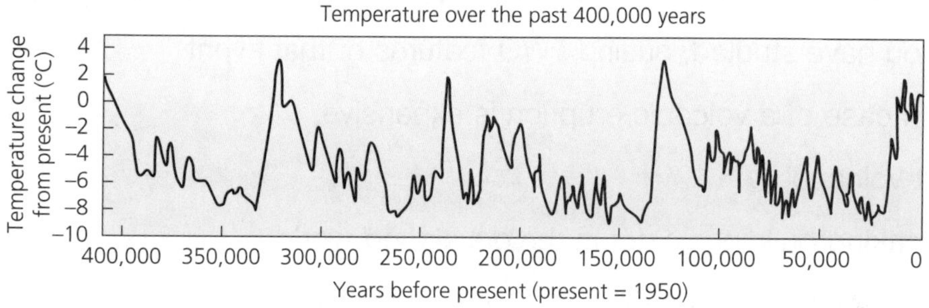

In recent times temperatures have varied by as much as 1.5 °C each side of the average. It only takes very small changes in average temperatures to make a great deal of difference to what you can grow and where you can grow it.

Figure 2 Temperature changes in more recent times

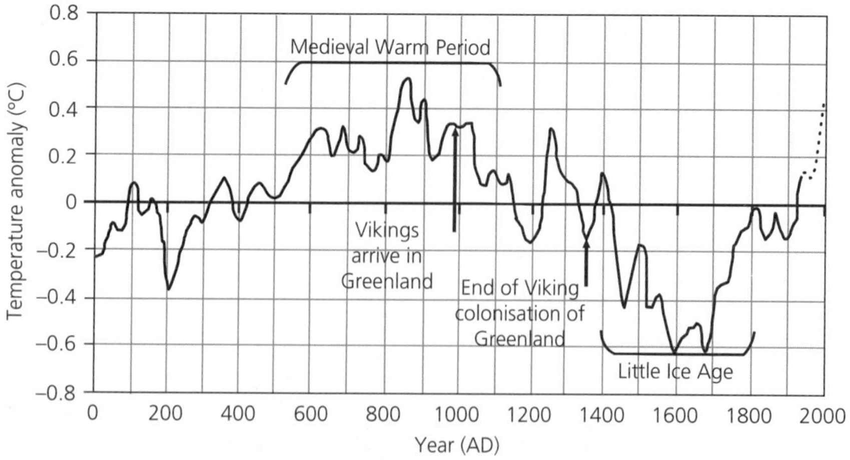

The causes of change

Revised

There are several theories about past **climate change**. It is possible that these processes operate either together, in which case climate change would be quite severe, or perhaps they 'pull' in opposite directions, in which case the changes would not be as large. The three most important global causes are:

1 **Volcanic eruptions**
- Large eruptions spew out vast quantities of dust and gases such as sulphur dioxide into the atmosphere.
- This blocks out or absorbs incoming solar radiation so the Earth cools.
- Examples include Mt Pinataubo in 1991, the Laki eruption in 1783 and Mt Toba 70,000 years ago, which some believe nearly finished off the human race altogether.

2 **Sunspot** activity
- Sunspots are darker areas on the Sun's surface – they are a sign of greater **solar activity**.
- They come and go in cycles of about 11 years.
- However, there are periods when very few sunspots were observed, such as 1645–1715.
- This period coincides with the 'Little Ice Age'.

3 Changes in the Earth's orbit and rotation (**Milankovitch mechanism**)
- The shape of the Earth's **orbit changes** (becoming more or less circular) over a period of 100,000 years – known as orbital eccentricity.
- The Earth 'wobbles' on its axis over a period of 26,000 years – known as **precession**.
- The tilt, or obliquity, of the axis varies between 21° and 24° over about 40,000 years.
- Taken together these effects change the amount of solar energy received at the Earth's surface.

Figure 3 The Milankovitch mechanism

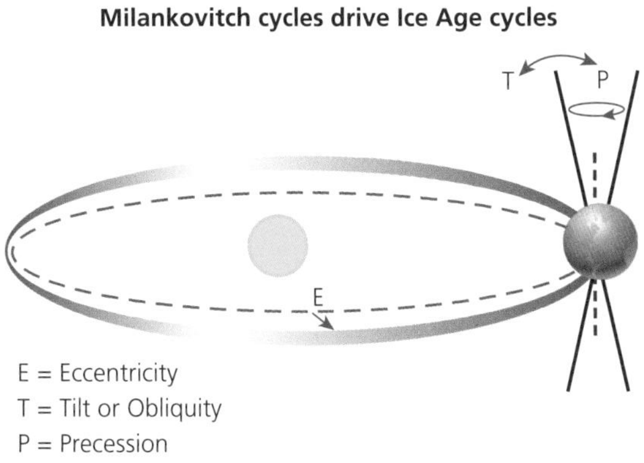

Other causes may be more local – for example, the **North Atlantic oscillation**:
- In Europe we are used to our winters being fairly mild because the wind is usually in the west and is warmed as it crosses the Atlantic.
- Occasionally this pattern weakens and European winters are dominated by cold air and easterly winds from Siberia.

Knowing the basics

All three reasons for climate change can operate together, making the planet hotter or colder, but might also cancel each other out.

Stretch and challenge

There is a lot of evidence that the oceans play a key role in controlling global temperatures and if this gets out of balance then change can accelerate.

Check your understanding

Tested

Identify three causes of past climate change.

The Little Ice Age

Revised

Past climate change can be both positive and negative. Colder weather would have reduced the harvest and led to famine and starvation in countries that today would be able to import food and simply turn the heating up; expensive but not fatal for most people. By contrast warmer periods have led to better harvests and more trade.

One of the best-known periods of climate change in the recent past is the so-called **Little Ice Age**, probably caused by changes in the North Atlantic oscillation as well as reduced sunspot activity. It lasted from about 1300 to as late as 1870 (see Figure 2) and average temperatures were at least 1 °C below those of today.

Impacts of the Little Ice Age included the following:

- The Baltic Sea froze over in winter, as did most of the rivers in Europe including the Thames.
- Sea ice, which today is far to the north, reached as far south as Iceland.
- Winters were much colder and longer, reducing the growing season by several weeks.
- These conditions led to widespread crop failure and famine.
- As a result, population declined sharply in some regions. For example, Iceland lost half of its population during the Little Ice Age.
- Remote areas such as Greenland were abandoned by settlers as survival became impossible (see Figure 4).
- The price of grain increased almost everywhere, leading to social unrest and revolt.
- Commercial vineyards vanished in England.
- Fishing was poor as the fish, such as cod, migrated south to find warmer water.
- Storminess and flooding increased.
- In mountainous regions the tree line and snowline dropped – some Scottish mountains were permanently covered with snow for several hundred years.
- **Glaciers** advanced in the Alps and northern Europe, overrunning towns and farms in the process.

Knowing the basics

Remember that climate change might bring benefits especially if temperatures get warmer in cold regions, such as Iceland.

Figure 4 An abandoned Viking settlement in Greenland

Check your understanding

Tested

Identify THREE pieces of evidence that the climate might have been colder in the past.

The impact on megafauna

Revised

An important lesson for humans is that past climate change led to major extinctions. There have been many such episodes – one of the largest, 250 million years ago, saw 93 per cent of all marine creatures wiped out.

The causes of these events probably vary but usually involve climate in some way. If the environment changes then not all living organisms can adapt and if they cannot adapt they will die out.

Figure 5 The impact of change

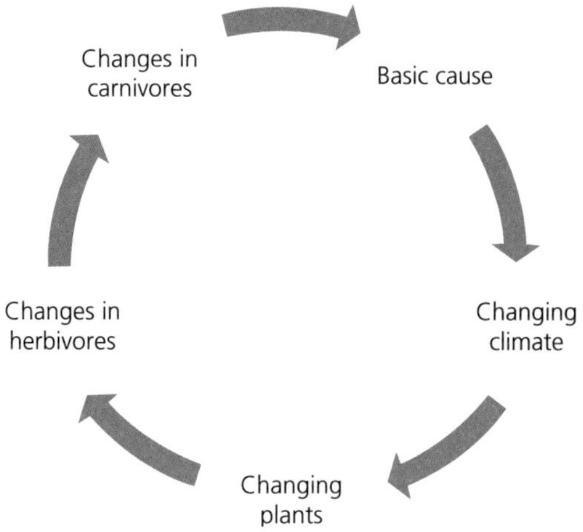

Knowing the basics

Extinctions take place when species do not have time to adapt.

Stretch and challenge

The most vulnerable species are at the top of the food chain because they depend on the all the other species for their existence. **Megafauna** are more vulnerable than insects.

Megafauna and the Ice Age

The climate change associated with the end of the **Ice Age** some 10,000–15,000 years ago saw temperatures rise by as much as 5 °C in a very short period (by geological standards) of 1000 years.

During this period a number of large animals, so-called **megafauna**, disappeared completely – as many as 130 species in all. Examples include giant beavers, mammoths and sabre-toothed tigers. There are three sets of explanations:

1 They could not cope with the climate change, with their preferred food – both plant and animal – disappearing; so they too died out.

2 Human beings, our ancestors, hunted them to extinction. We know for sure that we hunted these animals from the evidence of their remains.

3 A combination of 1 and 2 is always possible and maybe most likely.

The 'message' of this is clear. At the moment species are dying out at a faster rate than at any other time in the history of the planet, 1000 times faster than 'normal'.

exam tip

Some questions will ask you to 'Describe ONE ...' but have a two-mark tariff. Make sure that you develop your point rather than introduce a second reason.

The greenhouse effect

Revised

Greenhouse gases retain heat from the Sun that would otherwise be reflected from the Earth back into space. Without them the planet would be too cold to support life. Some scientists like to quote the 'Goldilocks Principle' when talking about the Earth's climate. It can be summed up as 'Venus is too hot, Mars is too cold, and Earth is just right'. Without greenhouse gases, as on Mars (surface temperature –53°C), life would never have arisen. With too much greenhouse gas, as on Venus (surface temperature +450°C), again life would not be possible.

- Solar energy passes through the atmosphere without having any real impact on it.
- About half of it is absorbed by the Earth – the rest is reflected back by clouds or the ground, absorbed by clouds or the upper atmosphere or simply scattered back to space.
- But the 51 per cent absorbed by the ground is radiated back into the atmosphere and this radiation is trapped by greenhouse gases.

Stretch and challenge

The Sun is so hot its energy is all at the short-wavelength end of the spectrum. The cooler Earth re-radiates energy at a longer wave – it is this long-wave radiation that is captured by greenhouse gases.

Greenhouse gases

There are several greenhouse gases, including water vapour, methane and nitrous oxide, but the one associated most with human activity is **carbon dioxide**.

Figure 6 Carbon dioxide gas and temperatures over the past 1000 years

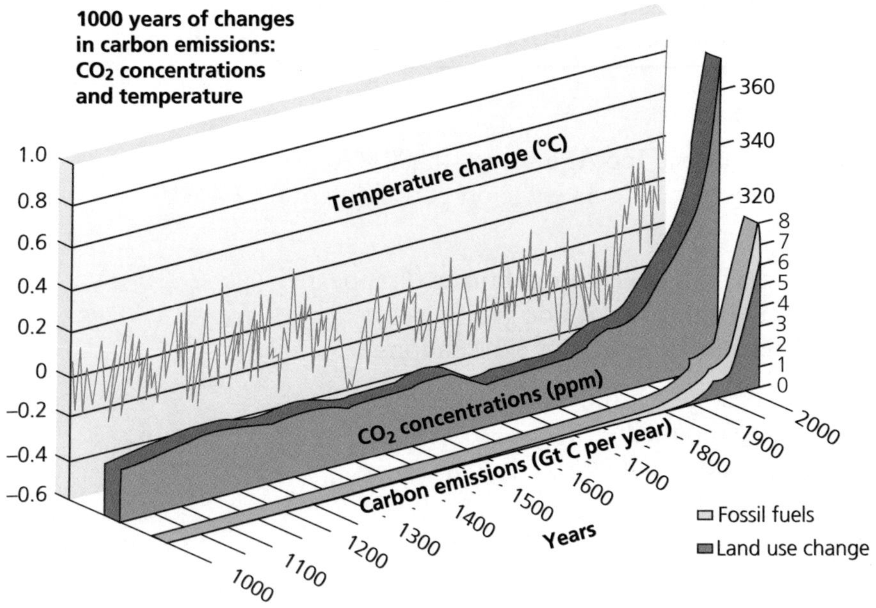

Recent changes in CO_2 are a result of burning fossil fuels such as gas, coal and, above all, oil. CO_2 is also created when making cement and steel. The largest contributing countries are:

1 China
2 USA
3 Russia
4 India
5 Japan

What we do and why we do it

Revised

Human activities have increased the amount of CO_2 produced and reduced the ability of the environment to absorb it. Since the **industrial revolution** the levels of all greenhouse gases have risen.

Year	1850	1950	Today
Carbon dioxide (ppm)	280	323	394
Methane (ppb)*	700	1430	1940
Nitrous oxide (ppm)	270	304	318

**Note that methane is measured in parts per billion (ppb) whereas the others are measured in parts per million (ppm).*

The majority of this increase is a result of activities in the developed world where each person produces between 10 and 25 tonnes a year of CO_2 alone. The poorest 25 per cent of humanity emit less than 2 per cent of the global total. That said, rapid industrialisation in India and China is raising their emissions too.

The main reasons for this increase are:

- energy supply (39 per cent of CO_2), which burns coal, gas and oil; most US and Chinese electricity is produced by burning coal
- transport (29 per cent of CO_2), which burns oil; 90 per cent of all journeys are powered by oil
- industry (17 per cent of CO_2) – making things uses energy and produces waste.

Other greenhouse gases have different origins:

- Nitrous oxide is produced by jet engines, fertilisers and sewage farms.
- Methane is most commonly associated with cows producing gas as they graze – about 200 litres of gas per day! With many more people eating meat, cattle numbers have doubled in 50 years.

Human activities also reduce the ability of the environment to absorb greenhouse gases, especially CO_2. The main cause of this is **deforestation**, which has two effects:

1 Burning forest to clear land produces CO_2.
2 Reducing the number of trees lowers the ability of the Earth to absorb CO_2.

Stretch and challenge

Water vapour is the most important greenhouse gas. We are some way from knowing exactly what happens to water vapour levels in the atmosphere as the planet warms, but it seems likely that they will increase.

What challenges might our future climate present us with?

The impact on global temperatures and sea level

Revised

Figure 6 (page 18) showed that global temperatures have risen quite sharply in the past 100 years. The vast majority of experts agree that greenhouse gases are directly linked to global temperature increases. So if we get the relationship between greenhouses gases and **global warming** correct, then models of how things might develop can be drawn up.

Figure 7 Predicted global temperature rise

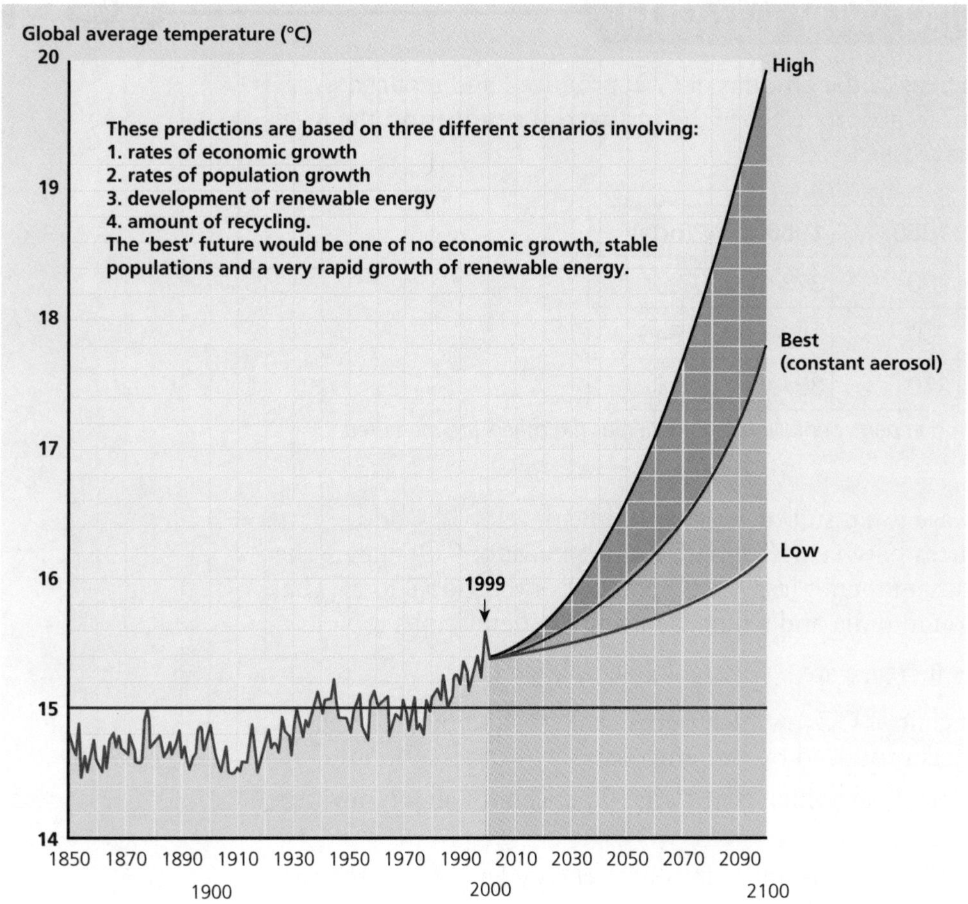

As Figure 7 shows, we cannot be certain about the future – these predictions range from an increase of 1 °C if we take action now to 6.4 °C if we do nothing.

Knowing the basics

The climate has certainly got warmer – the causes are a little more controversial.

Sea-level change

The most obvious impact of rising temperatures is rising sea level. Sea level has risen by about 200 mm since 1870 (about the width of this page). This has come about for two main reasons:

1 Melting **ice caps** and glaciers. Most ice is held in Greenland and Antarctica (99 per cent of all freshwater) – there are 30 million km^3 of ice in Antarctica alone.

2 As temperatures rise so water expands – this **thermal expansion** takes place independently of melting ice.

There could be a rise in sea level of between 300 mm and 1000 mm depending on how we tackle global warming.

Stretch and challenge

Remember that a rise in temperature might lead to other factors accelerating the release of greenhouse gases – for example, by 'unlocking' methane trapped in permanently frozen ground in large areas of Canada and Siberia.

What futures?

Revised

Just as past climate change offered challenges (see pages 16 and 17), so will future climate change.

For this section you will need to include case-study details of your developing country to add to those that you will have covered in class for the UK. These need to be put into two main categories:

1. Impacts on the economy and the people
2. Impacts on the environment.

exam tip

Be careful with the word 'environment' in questions – it means the *natural* environment.

Impact	The UK	Developing country
Environmental impact: Rising sea level	Low lying areas of East Anglia might cost too much to protect. Risks of flooding in London will increase	
Environmental impact: Changing temperatures and rainfall	Temperature rise and changing rainfall patterns might cause drought in some parts of the country making water scarce. Heatwaves, such as that of 2003, will become more common	
Environmental impact: Wild weather	Increased storminess might mean more erosion on some coasts, such as Holderness, and more river flooding. Storms, such as those in 1987 and 1990, might become much more frequent	
Environmental impact: Changing ecosystems	Certain species of birds and even animals might return while others will disappear. Changing sea temperatures will affect the number and quality of fish species off our shores	
Economic impact: Agriculture	Farming patterns are likely to change – perhaps more vines, more maize and other crops replacing barley and orchard crops	
Economic impact: Industry and services	A risk to London would pose a serious threat to the UK economy with its heavy dependence on finance and business services	
Economic impact: Tourism	Tourism could benefit with less need to travel overseas to seek the Sun. On the other hand, the Scottish skiing industry is likely to disappear	

Exam focus

1 Using Figure 1, describe the pattern of temperature changes over the past 400,000 years. [3]

2 Using Figure 2, identify the correct answer. [1]

A. The Medieval Warm Period lasted 600 years.

B. The Little Ice Age lasted 500 years.

C. The Little Ice Age ended in AD1700.

D. The medieval warm period started in AD800.

3 Explain ONE way in which volcanic eruptions can change global temperatures. [2]

4 Describe ONE way in which the orbit of the Earth varies. [2]

5 What was the Little Ice Age? [2]

6 Outline TWO possible impacts of colder average temperatures on farming. [4]

7 Which of the following best describes the extinction of megafauna? [1]

A. When species migrate to avoid cold weather.

B. When large plants cannot survive colder conditions.

C. When large animals cannot evolve fast enough and become extinct.

D. When numbers of large animals increase because of warmer climate.

8 Name TWO species of megafauna. [2]

9 Explain why greenhouse gases are vital for life. [4]

10 Identify THREE greenhouse gases. [3]

11 Using the table on page 19, compare changes in the quantities of CO_2 and methane between 1850 and today. [4]

12 Outline ONE reason why developed countries produce more greenhouse gases than developing countries. [2]

13 Using Figure 7, describe the forecasts for future global temperature changes. [3]

14 Outline ONE reason why predicting future global temperature changes is difficult. [2]

15 For a named developed country, explain TWO possible impacts of climate change on its economy. [4]

16 For a named developing country, describe TWO possible impacts of climate change on its environment. [4]

Answers online Online

Chapter 3 Battle for the Biosphere

What is the value of the biosphere?

Biomes and their distribution

Revised

A **biome** is a large-scale **ecosystem** – that is to say, a community of plants and animals. Biomes often blend into one another – for example, tropical rainforest gives way bit by bit, mile by mile, to savannah despite the lines on the map appearing to mark clear boundaries.

Figure 1 Global biomes

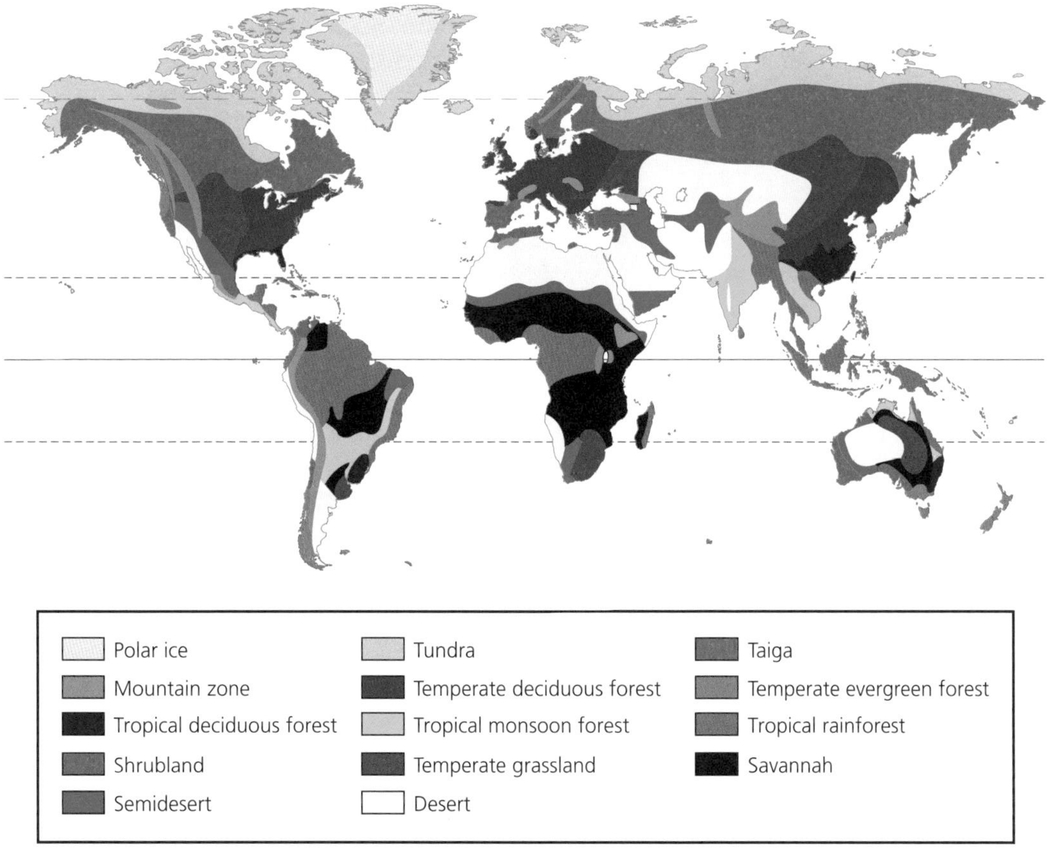

Stretch and challenge

Remember that biomes do vary. Tropical rainforest in Malaysia isn't exactly the same as tropical rainforest in Brazil – the species of plants and animals are very different, although many of the processes are similar.

The main biomes include:

- tropical rainforest found on either side of the equator – a very 'rich' environment where wet and hot conditions encourage all-year-round growth of plants
- desert that is found in the tropics – it is very dry and plants have to adapt to survive with deep roots and thick skins
- temperate deciduous forest found in higher latitudes – trees lose their leaves in the autumn to conserve energy
- taiga (coniferous forest), dominant from 60° northwards for many hundreds of kilometres – it is so cold in winter that trees have evolved needle leaves and waxy resin to reduce heat and moisture loss.

exam tip

Remember that questions that ask for 'located' or 'named' examples expect you to do just that and preferably not at the 'In Africa…' scale.

exam tip

Examination questions will often ask you to 'Describe ONE factor that…' Make sure that you don't offer two or three factors – you'll only be judged on one of them.

The influence of climate, altitude and soils on biomes

Revised

Biomes have developed over very long periods of time and, generally, the web of plants and animals that are associated with particular biomes are a result of variations in:

1. temperature
2. rainfall
3. altitude
4. geology and soils.

Where precipitation is quite high (over 1000 mm) and distributed fairly evenly throughout the year, temperature is the most important factor in biome location. It is not simply a matter of average temperature, but includes other factors such as:

- whether it ever freezes
- length of the growing season (average temperature needs to be above 6 °C for plants to grow).

If there is ample rainfall, we find four characteristic biomes. In order, from the equator, they are:

- tropical rainforest
- temperate deciduous forest
- taiga
- tundra.

Stretch and challenge

The hotter and wetter the climate, the more productive is the ecosystem, with more species of both **fauna** and **flora**.

The other major biomes are controlled not so much by temperature but by the amount and seasonal distribution of rainfall. Rainfall generally reduces as one moves inland away from the oceans.

How much falls and when it falls controls whether the biome will be:

- temperate rainforest
- grassland or
- desert.

Altitude is considered to be a local factor because it controls both temperature and rainfall. There are glaciers on the equator and in a country such as Bolivia one can climb from tropical rainforest up through temperate forest to deserts and tundra before reaching the ice in the high Andes. Average temperature falls by about 1°C for every 200 m of altitude.

Soils are also important locally. Thin soils will not support much plant life and slopes and geology will influence this.

Check your understanding

Tested

1. Define the term 'biome'.
2. Name TWO examples of biomes.

Biosphere services

Revised

The **biosphere** provides many **services** for the planet, acting as a life support system for the other spheres.

Services provided include:

- regulation of climate – temperature and rainfall patterns
- regulation of atmospheric gases – especially levels of CO_2 and oxygen
- water regulation through controlling the flow of water
- water purification – water is filtered naturally through plants
- soil formation and development – rotting vegetation is recycled and used continually unless people intervene.

Another set of 'cultural services' is also provided, including:

- spiritual and religious effects
- recreation and ecotourism
- inspiration for writers, poets, artists and musicians
- educational resources in the natural environment
- a 'sense of place' – many people feel at home in certain wilderness environments.

The most important of these is probably the regulation of atmospheric gases.

Figure 2 The carbon cycle

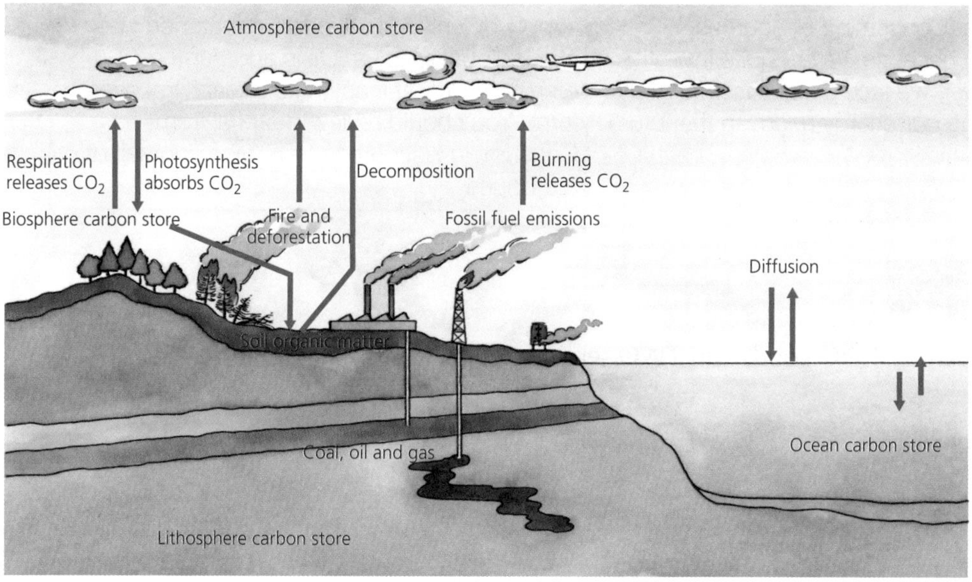

- Plants absorb CO_2 and produce oxygen.
- Plants use water for growth but also transpire water back into the atmosphere.
- Vegetation regulates temperature.

Knowing the basics

The ocean is the largest **carbon store**.

Stretch and challenge

The ability of the ocean to absorb CO_2 decreases as the ocean warms up.

Check your understanding

Tested

Outline ONE way in which the biosphere controls the climate.

Goods from the biosphere

Revised

The biosphere also produces countless **goods** for people. Human existence depends upon these goods. Although we modify them and combine them to make new products, all life is dependent on these basic resources.

Resource	Comment	Example
Food	Only a very few people depend ***directly*** on the biosphere today. The nearest most people get to 'hunter-gathering' is picking blackberries or shooting rabbits	All that we eat has its origin in the natural world. 95 per cent of human food comes from 30 plants, and 75 per cent from only eight of these. These crops, such as rice, wheat and maize, are all descended from wild grasses and other plants
Medicines	If we continue to destroy plant species and animal species at current rates we are losing the potential to cure diseases. We have embarked on very significant research mapping genomes of plants and animals – we have no idea what benefits these might bring for human health and prosperity	Quinine is the best-known example of a 'natural' medicine; this treatment for malaria is derived from the cinchona tree. Rosy periwinkle, a plant from Madagascar, gives us two very important cancer-fighting medicines: vinblastine and vincristine. Vinblastine has helped increase the chances of surviving childhood leukaemia from 10 per cent to 95 per cent, while vincristine is used to treat Hodgkin's lymphoma
Raw materials	We have never run out of a resource (look at Consuming Resources, Unit 2) because we are quite inventive – however, we face serious issues over meeting our energy needs in the future	The most basic raw material is water, the supply of which is seriously threatened in many global regions. Oil is another that is running short, at least in its cheaply recovered form. You should review material from Consuming Resources to remind yourself of the issues

Check your understanding

Tested

For ONE named biome identify TWO goods and TWO services produced.

How have humans affected the biosphere and how might it be conserved?

Destroying the biosphere – part 1

Revised

There is an obvious conflict between preserving the environment and economic development. The economic development of countries such as the UK involved major damage to the biosphere as forests were cleared, species wiped out and water and air polluted. Today the rapid economic growth in countries such as China, India and Brazil is also bringing changes – some of these are listed below.

Tar-sands in Canada

In a world short of oil the sticky mixture of tar and sand found in Alberta province is bringing wealth to the companies extracting the oil and the Canadian government. Covering over 140,000 km^2, an area larger than England, the sands hold reserves of 1.75 trillion barrels. To get at this huge resource the forests that cover the region have to be stripped away and vast quantities of water and natural gas have to be used to extract the oil.

Mountain-top removal in the USA

American coal companies use mountain-top removal in the Appalachian Mountains of eastern USA. As the name suggests, the technique involves slicing off the top of the mountain, having removed the overlying forest, and discarding the waste into the valley below – all in order to expose the coal, which can be removed by machines. The rivers and water table are degraded, as are the fauna and flora.

Shrimp and prawn farms in India

In many parts of south and east Asia, prawn farms are a common sight along the coast. Once a local means of adding some protein to the diet, it is now a global enterprise worth over $6 billion. In many places, including the coast of Andhra Pradesh in India, the environment has changed considerably. During the 1980s and 1990s, about 35 per cent of the world's mangrove forests vanished, with shrimp farming a major cause of this, accounting for over a third of the destruction according to one study. The removal of mangroves reduces **biodiversity** and has a major impact on coastal protection.

Palm oil in Malaysia

Malaysia and Indonesia are responsible for about 80 per cent of global palm oil production, most of which is used for **biofuel**. **Deforestation** and biodiversity decline occur as the land is cleared to plant only palm trees. Some environmental campaigners also argue that this land-use change adds significantly to greenhouse gas emissions.

Stretch and challenge

It is too easy to think that destruction of the environment is something that happens in the developing world. Two of these examples are from the developed world. It is also worth remembering that environmental changes such as prawn farms or palm oil plantations are to satisfy demand from rich countries.

exam tip

The command word 'outline' steers you to give a brief overview and not just to 'name' or 'identify'.

Destroying the biosphere – part 2

Revised

Human activity alters the **biosphere** indirectly as well as directly. When we impact on climate and the composition of the atmosphere, we impact on the biosphere too.

Figure 3 Indirect impacts on the biosphere

Climate change
- Increased greenhouse gas emissions
- Increases in particles and pollutants

Impacts
- Changes in weather patterns
- Changes in temperature
- Changes in sea level and temperature
- More extreme weather events

Effect on biosphere
- Less plankton and shellfish
- Migration of animals
- Species stress and extinctions

Knowing the basics

Changes in the biosphere are an inevitable result of climate change, especially when the change is rapid.

Stretch and challenge

The damage to the biosphere is obvious – however, in times of economic crisis it scarcely features in government policies.

'We now face losing marine species and entire marine ecosystems, such as coral reefs, within a single generation', according to a study by 27 experts presented to the United Nations in 2011. 'Unless action is taken now, the consequences of our activities are at a high risk of causing, through the combined effects of climate change, over-exploitation, pollution and habitat loss, the next globally significant extinction event in the ocean', the report said.

Three main threats to the biosphere have been identified:

1. increased temperatures in our oceans
2. **acidification** due to more CO_2 being absorbed by our oceans
3. **anoxia** – reduction of oxygen in our oceans.

The first two of these are indirect results of climate change – the third is a result of discharging pollutants and fertilisers into oceans.

Many scientists think that previous **mass extinctions** of ocean life were caused by changes such as these. If the oceans 'die', the impact on the atmosphere could threaten all planetary life.

Biosphere conservation

Revised

There are many examples of attempts at biosphere **conservation**. These range in scale from global to local. Listed below are three examples of such schemes plus space for you complete brief details of your own examples should you have studied different schemes.

Scale	Details	Your example
Global	The Ramsar Convention is an international treaty between over 160 countries that aims to conserve wetlands and encourage their **sustainable use**. It aims to slow down the loss of wetlands now and in the future, recognising the fundamental ecological functions of wetlands and their economic, cultural, scientific and recreational value. It is named after the town of Ramsar in Iran	
National	National Parks were formed in the UK in order to preserve landscapes. Unlike US National Parks they are not owned by the people but have strict planning laws that aim to preserve valuable landscapes that include human as well as natural environments. The first UK National Park was the Lake District. There are now 15 of them belonging to a global family of over 113,000 protected areas, covering 149 million km^2 or 6 per cent of the Earth's surface	
Local	The Biosphere Conservancy in Mexico works with local communal lands called ejidos. The ejidos consist of 350 families and comprise about 30,000 hectares of forestland. The Conservancy helped the ejidos get established with proper land ownership rights. In 2007–2008 it helped build a bridge that allows year-round access to the forest, making the ejidos' sustainable forestry operation more competitive and profitable by allowing the sale of softwoods	

exam tip

Be careful with scales – if you are asked for a local-scale example then make sure that is what you provide.

Being sustainable at a local scale

Revised

Sustainable development is not easy to achieve. Almost inevitably the use of resources is likely to bring economic benefits but be costly for the environment. **Sustainable management** is not quite the same thing as sustainable development in which the priority is to meet the needs of the poor. Sustainable management generally involves:

- conserving the environment so that it has time to regenerate for future generations
- avoidance of bad practices that damage the ecosystem for the profit of people who do not live locally
- provision for local people, especially the poor and disadvantaged
- education of local people so they feel involved in the project as the most important **stakeholders.**

You will have studied an example of local, small-scale biosphere management. You need to be able to answer a question about what makes this project sustainable.

Named project	
Management technique 1	Why sustainable?
Management technique 2	Why sustainable?
Management technique 3	Why sustainable?

exam tip

Always look at the number of marks awarded. All questions worth less than 6 marks are point marked. One point = one mark.

Exam focus

1 Using Figure 1, describe the distribution of tropical rainforests. [3]

2 Using Figure 1, identify which of the following statements about the distribution of taiga is correct. [1]

A. It is mainly found close to the equator.

B. Most of it is found in North and South America.

C. It is common in Canada and Russia.

D. It is never found in Asia.

3 Outline how altitude affects climate. [2]

4 Outline ONE reason why the average temperature helps explain the distribution of biomes. [2]

5 Describe TWO services provided by biomes. [4]

6 Explain how the biosphere helps to control the Earth's climate. [4]

7 Identify ONE way in which biomes contribute to food production. [1]

8 Identify ONE way in which biomes contribute to medicine. [1]

9 For a named biome, describe how resource extraction has contributed to its destruction. [4]

10 Outline ONE reason why people in developing countries find it hard to protect their environment. [2]

11 Name TWO threats to the health of our oceans. [2]

12 For ONE named threat, explain how marine life is threatened. [3]

13 Outline ONE way in which national governments can help protect the environment. [2]

14 Suggest why global agreement is needed to help protect the environment. [2]

15 Outline TWO features of sustainable management of the environment. [4]

16 For a named management scheme, describe how it helps make a local area more sustainable. [4]

Answers online Online

Chapter 4 Water World

Why is water important to the health of the planet?

Water on the planet

Revised

Figure 1 Global water supply

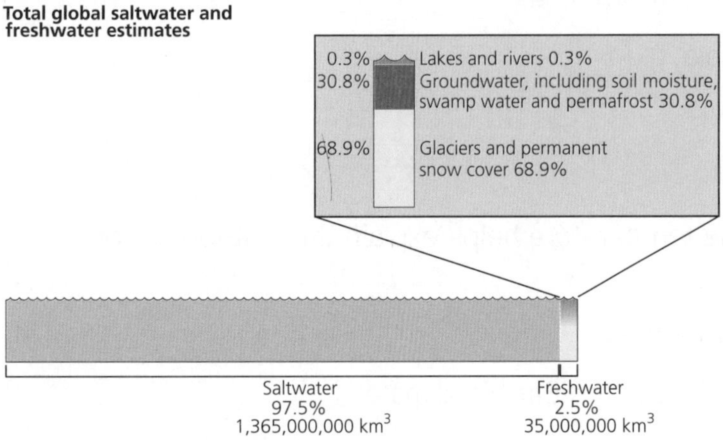

Figure 1 shows the water stores on Earth – the so-called **hydrosphere**. Most of this global water is held in the oceans. The other major stores of water are:

- glaciers and snow cover
- groundwater
- lakes and rivers.

Water is part of a closed system. There is a limited amount of water on Earth and although we don't really know where it came from we know that it cannot escape into space or leak away into the crust. So the water that you drink has been drunk before, probably many times, and of course been returned to the system. The molecules don't disappear but are recycled through a number of processes.

This recycling mechanism is known as the **hydrological cycle**. Water circulates through this via the biosphere (especially plants), **lithosphere** (water is stored in the ground and runs over it and through it) and back to the atmosphere.

Knowing the basics

The vast majority of water is in the oceans. The vast majority of fresh water is held in ice sheets.

Check your understanding

Tested

Identify THREE stores of water.

The workings of the hydrological cycle

Figure 2 The hydrological cycle

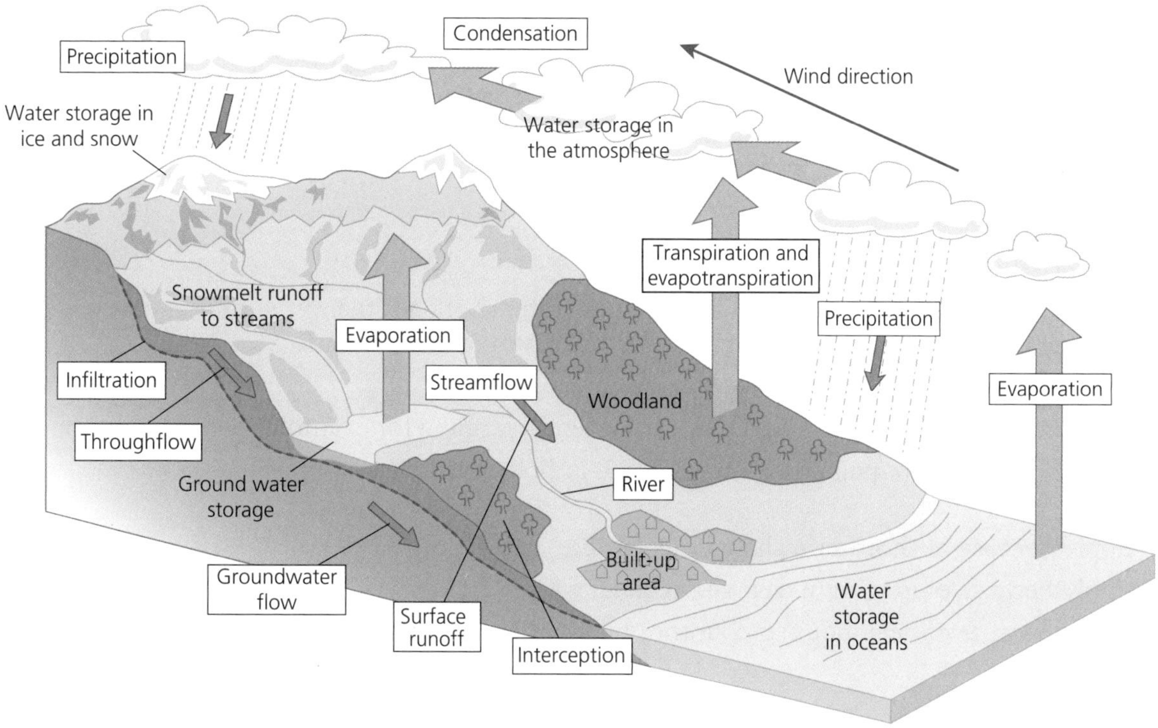

Figure 2 shows the hydrological cycle. This is composed of stores (see Figure 1 for more details) and a set of processes which transfer water from one store to another. Remember that the vast majority of water is held in the oceans.

Essentially these stores control the climate on Earth. Small changes in the temperature and the chemistry of ocean water affect the atmosphere and so our climate. The key processes are as follows:

- **Evaporation** – this is the transfer of water from its liquid state to its gaseous state, water vapour. The process depends on temperature – the higher the temperature the more evaporation takes place.
- **Transpiration** and **evapotranspiration** – this is similar to evaporation but involves liquid water lost from plants returning to the atmosphere as a gas. Plants 'breathe out' water but also lose it by evaporation from surfaces such as leaves; hence evapotranspiration.
- **Condensation** – this is where water vapour (a gas) becomes liquid water again. This happens when air containing water vapour is cooled. The result is clouds or, at a low level, fog and mist.
- **Precipitation** – not all clouds give rain but when the conditions are right, water droplets in clouds (which are microscopic) become water drops or, more often, snowflakes and gravity does the rest – more often than not the snowflakes melt as they fall through warmer air.
- **Surface runoff** and **groundwater flow** – when precipitation reaches the ground it either soaks into the ground (**infiltration**) and then moves downhill under the surface as **groundwater flow** or, when the ground is saturated with water or too compact to allow water to infiltrate, it runs off the surface into rivers.
- **Streamflow** – some groundwater flow and surface runoff will reach rivers and streams where it generally continues its route towards the sea or ocean.

exam tip

These processes are important and questions about them are very common.

The impact of unreliable and/or insufficient water supply

Revised

Human beings are very good at adapting. People can survive and flourish in a wide variety of climates and in environments that seem quite challenging to those of us who are used to expecting water to come out every time we turn on a tap. Knowing that shortages might be coming allows people to change their behaviour to adapt. The most difficult problems arise when:

- shortages are unexpected
- there are long-term changes in both demand and supply.

Some parts of the world are obviously more at risk from water shortages than others. In many of these regions a combination of factors have come together to cause rainfall to become insufficient:

- rising demand because of changing land use – commercial farming for example
- rising demand because of population increase – true in both Australia and the Sahel region
- falling supply because of short-term changes in climate – see Figure 3
- falling supply because of long-term changes in climate – see Figure 3
- falling supply because of neighbouring countries taking more water from rivers.

Figure 3 Changing rainfall in the Sahel region

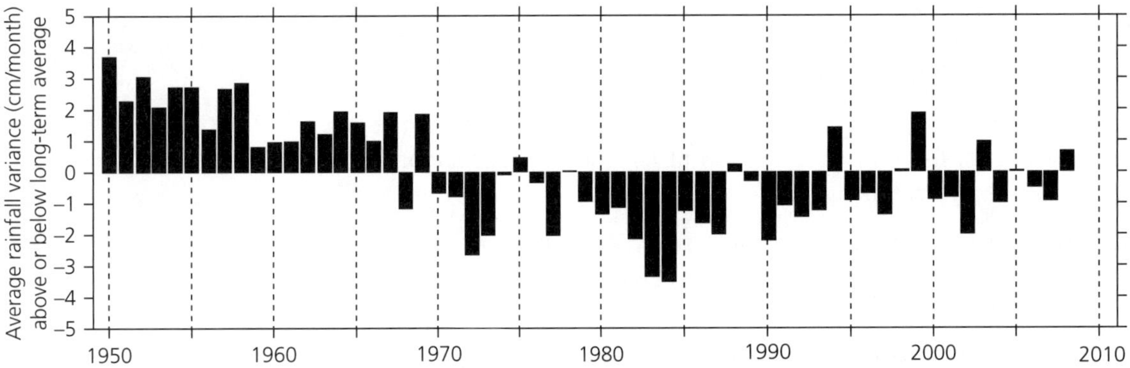

Fill in the spaces below to remind yourself about the details of your own case study of the impact of unreliable and insufficient water supply. Aim to make at least four points about the impact and try to include both insufficiency (not enough rain) and unreliability (the problem of *when* it falls).

Named area	Description of climate	Impact of climate on people
Location: Details of place:	Rainfall: Recent changes? Reliable? Sufficient?	Problems of insufficiency: Problems of unreliability:

Stretch and challenge

Remember that even developed countries in wet climate regions have water supply issues. Singapore has to import water from its neighbour, Malaysia.

The impact of climate change on vulnerable regions

Revised

Figure 4 Increasing water stress – the world of water in 2070

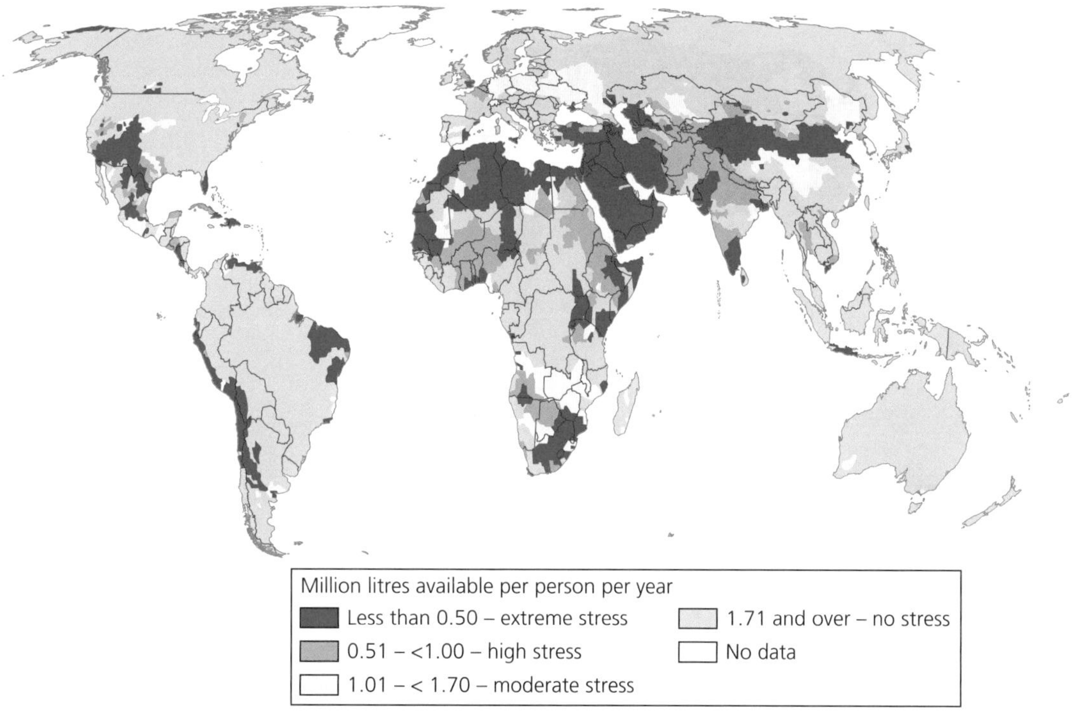

The impact of climate change is likely to bring more rain to some areas but less to others. In other global regions temperatures might change in such a way as to increase rates of evaporation.

So the stores and processes in the hydrological cycle will obviously be altered – but not in ways that we can predict for certain.

exam tip

To answer questions on this topic you should use the case study you know for sub-topic 3 and add in details of possible future climate change.

Figure 4 shows some of the possible changes to **water stress** by 2070. The amount of water used per person is not just the water that people drink and wash with, but includes water required to grow food, make goods and provide services.

When this measure of water per person falls below around 1400 litres a day it is defined as 'extreme stress'. The areas most likely to experience increasing water stress are the red areas across North Africa and through a broad sweep of the Middle East and into central Asia. The factors that lead to the increase in stress are:

- decreasing rainfall
- less reliable rainfall
- increasing temperatures
- increasing population
- increasing industrialisation.

Check your understanding

Tested

What do you understand by the term 'vulnerable region'?

How can water resources be sustainably managed?

Quality not quantity

Revised

Figure 5 Global availability of fresh drinking water

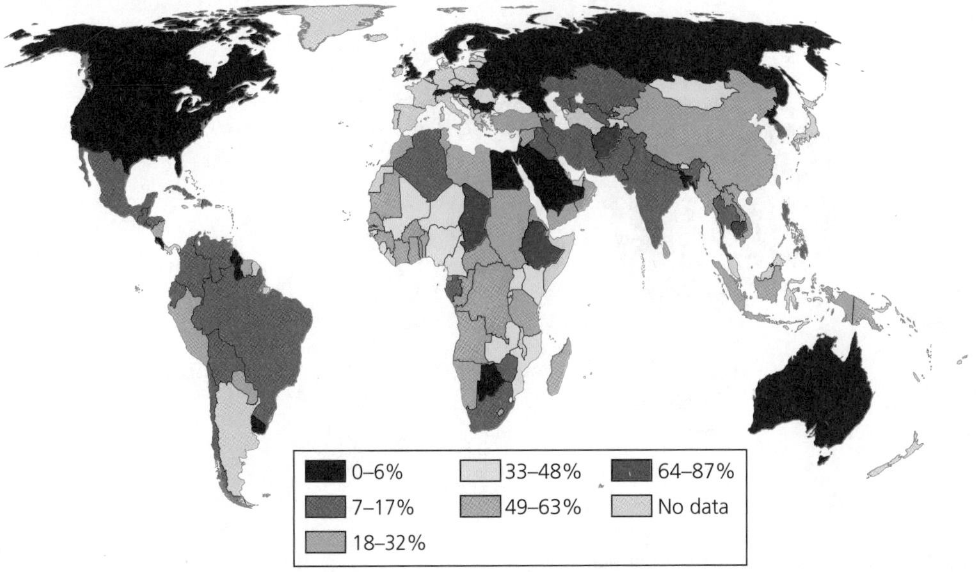

Figure 5 shows the percentage of the population who cannot access fresh drinking water. This is defined as at least 20 litres of drinking water being available within 2 km of where one lives. It is worth noting that:

- Africa has the worst record for this especially in the Sahel region south of the Sahara
- there are 'black spots' elsewhere, in Asia especially
- even the rapidly industrialising China still has between 18 per cent and 32 per cent without access to fresh water.

Water **pollution** in the developing world is almost always due to untreated sewage getting into local water supplies. More than 5 million people die each year as a result of water-borne diseases.

Water is also polluted by industrial and agricultural waste, especially in the developed world and **NIC**s. Examples are listed in the following table.

Source of pollution	Impacts and example
Toxic waste from mines	Heap-leach mining uses sodium cyanide, which can run off into river water and groundwater, e.g. Fort Belknap (USA). Many US states now ban this method but it is common in NICs
Plant fertilisers	Nitrates run off into rivers and lakes (and the ocean) causing **eutrophication** which kills off animals because they are deprived of oxygen
Chemical waste	Water consumed by people in China contains dangerous levels of arsenic, fluorine and sulphates, often discharged by factories. Of China's 1.3 billion people, 980 million drink water every day that is partly polluted
Radioactive waste	Nuclear waste can remain dangerous for many thousands of years. Storing it deep in the ground is risky because of both the time involved and the chance of leaks

exam tip

Questions that ask you to describe distributions on a map expect you to give a 'word picture' of what you are looking at.

Check your understanding

Tested

Identify TWO ways in which water quality might be improved.

Human interference

Revised

To revise this section you need to have some details of various ways in which human actions have disrupted the water supply. Disruption might involve:

- changing land use, such as deforestation
- taking too much groundwater (over-**abstraction**)
- **reservoir** construction.

For at least TWO of these you should have your own located details. The table below provides details of ONE of these; for at least one of the others complete the boxes to supply the facts, figures and ideas that you might need to answer a question on this topic.

Type of interference	Details	Impact on water supply
Deforestation	**Where?** Alberta in Canada **When?** Now **How/why?** The trees are being removed to expose the tar-sands below for mining. This is a source of oil. So far, the industry has removed about 389 km^2 of boreal forest (taiga)	Every day, about 1 million tonnes of the sand is dug and transported to be washed with about 200,000 tonnes of water. The water is then heated in order to extract the bitumen. It takes about three barrels of fresh water from the Athabasca River to produce just one barrel of oil. The industry uses more water per year than the entire city of Calgary, the largest city in Alberta. In return, one barrel of oil produces about two barrels of toxic water. The waste is pumped into dozens of holding lakes known as 'tailings ponds'. Some of these massive man-made lakes are dozens of kilometres across
Over-abstraction of groundwater	**Where?** **When?** **How/why?**	
Reservoir building	**Where?** **When?** **How/why?**	

exam tip

It's a good idea to double up here – you have to know a case study of a large water management scheme for sub-topic 7 so why not include brief details for this section too?

The costs and benefits of large-scale water management projects

Revised

Big dams have been popular with governments for many years. They are multi-purpose in that they are designed to meet several different needs. These include:

- flood control for areas downstream of the dam
- a supply of fresh water for agriculture, industry and domestic consumption
- a supply of power for **hydroelectricity**.

Large-scale water management projects differ in detail but have some common costs and benefits – the table below has included these but it is left to you to complete the details with your chosen case study.

	General points	**Case study points** **Chosen case study:**
Costs	• Controlled by central government • Expensive • Loss of local land/habitat etc. • Local people displaced and/or ignored • Pollution problems in lake • Possible sustainability issues – will it last? • Changing local ecosystem?	
Benefits	• Power generation • Attraction of industry for development • Flood control • Improved water supply • Possible leisure facility and tourism • Better food resources – fish? • Changing local ecosystem?	

Stretch and challenge

Remember that the people who gain from large-scale projects may not live close to the project itself. They don't suffer from any of the costs as a result.

Small-scale solutions to water management issues

Revised

Small-scale water management projects are sometimes funded by government but also by NGOs. They are usually:

- bottom-up projects controlled by the local community
- relatively cheap and easy to set up
- easy to maintain using only simple (**intermediate**) **technology**
- addressing local issues, especially water quality.

The table below contains one example. Add in another example of a small-scale sustainable water management project if you have one.

Scheme	How does it work?	Possible drawbacks?
Rainwater harvesting	Storing rainwater from rooftop runoff in jars is a cheap means of obtaining high-quality drinking water. Before the introduction of jars for rainwater storage, many communities had no means of protecting drinking water from waste and mosquito infestation. The jars come in various capacities, from 100 to 3000 litres and are equipped with lid, tap and drain. The most popular size is 2000 litres, which is cheap to buy and holds sufficient rainwater for a six-person household during the dry season, lasting up to six months.	Jars can be too expensive for some households, so technical assistance can be given to help make them locally, which encourages villagers to work together. This is environmentally appropriate technology which is easy to learn. In those villages that do not have enough labour for making water jars, access to loan funds is arranged to help villagers purchase them.
Second example:		

Knowing the basics

Most projects have winners and losers; positive things happen but so do negative things.

exam tip

Make sure that you get the scale right – if you are asked for a small-scale example then make sure that is what you provide.

Exam focus

1 Using Figure 1, describe the main global stores of water. [3]

2 Using Figure 1, identify which of the following statements about water stores is correct. [1]

A. Groundwater is the largest freshwater store.

B. 2.5 per cent of global water is fresh water.

C. There is more water in glaciers than in the oceans.

D. There is over 40 million km^3 of fresh water.

3 Name THREE processes that take place in the hydrological cycle. [3]

4 Describe how water is transferred from the Earth's surface to the atmosphere. [4]

5 Using Figure 3, describe the variations in annual rainfall shown. [4]

6 Outline ONE reason why demand for water may have risen. [2]

7 Using Figure 4, describe the distribution of areas of extreme water stress in Africa. [3]

8 Identify THREE reasons why water shortages might increase in the future. [3]

9 Using Figure 5, identify which of the following statements is correct. [1]

A. Over 33 per cent of South Americans cannot access fresh water.

B. Many parts of Australia have limited access to fresh water.

C. Water quality in North America is generally good.

D. Improving water quality is a feature of South Asia.

10 Outline ONE way in which resource extraction can affect water quality. [2]

11 Name THREE ways in which human actions have disrupted water supplies. [3]

12 For ONE human action explain its impact on the water supply. [4]

13 Outline ONE benefit of large dams for a country or region. [2]

14 For a named large-scale water management project, explain why it had both costs and benefits. [4]

15 For a named small-scale water management project, describe the benefits to the local population. [4]

16 Explain why both large-scale and small-scale water management projects have drawbacks. [4]

Answers online Online

Section B Small-scale Dynamic Planet

Chapter 5 Coastal Change and Conflict

How are different coastlines produced by physical processes?

Contrasting coasts

Revised

Coastal zones are dynamic areas, they change. Coastal zones vary according to:

- the processes that take place – how powerful are the waves?
- the type of rock in the area – how resistant is it to **erosion**?

You should have studied two contrasting coasts – one dominated by **soft rock**, one dominated by more resistant **hard rock**.

Stretch and challenge

Remember that the resistance of rock is not just a matter of its hardness – it is also how jointed and fractured it is. A shattered rock, even a hard one, will erode quite quickly.

Add details about your sections of coastline to this table.

General points	Your case studies
Hard rock coast	
• Cliffs tend to be high • Cliffs tend to be nearly vertical • Cliffs tend to retreat by rockfall • Features such as **caves**, **arches**, **stacks** and **stumps** • **Wave-cut platforms** as cliffs retreat • Beaches often stony	Rock type: Location: Details:
Soft rock coast	
• Cliffs either low or missing altogether • Cliffs gently sloping • Cliffs retreat by **sliding** and **slumping** • No stacks or stumps, caves rare • Wave-cut platforms unusual • Beaches often sandy	Rock type: Location: Details:

Erosional landforms

Marine processes include:

- **hydraulic action** – the force of water striking cliffs and often forcing air into cracks and crevices so fracturing the rock
- **abrasion** – rock and sand thrown with force against cliffs and dragged by waves across platforms will wear these surfaces away
- **attrition** – the rocks 'thrown' at cliffs and dragged across platforms will themselves be worn down and broken up.

Cliffs are formed by:

- erosion at the base by waves exploiting softer patches of material or fractures in the rock
- the undermining of the coast causing rockfall or slumping
- **weathering** and exposure to rainfall, so material is loosened and gravity removes it.

Concordant and discordant coasts

Revised

Figure 1 The Purbeck coast

This section is **concordant** with the geology running parallel to the coastline. The best known features here are those found at Lulworth Cove – see below.

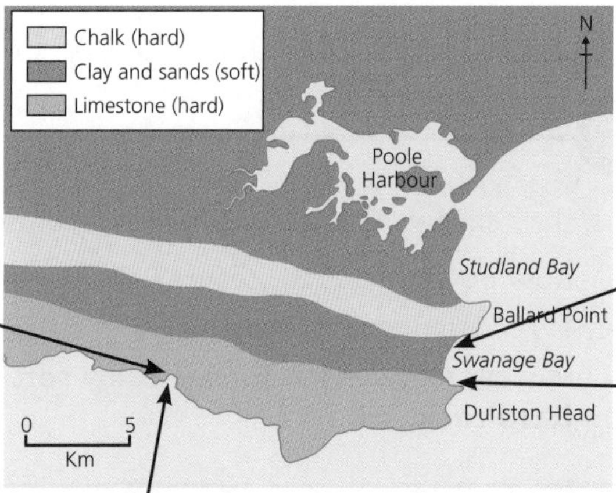

This section is **discordant** with the geology running at right angles to the coastline. The best known features here are those found at Swanage Bay and Studland Bay – see below.

Figure 2 Lulworth Cove

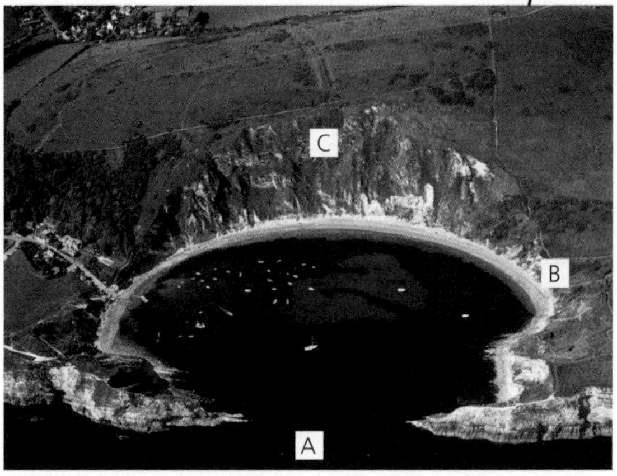

The rocks run parallel to the coast.

At Lulworth either coastal erosion or river erosion has broken through the resistant limestone at A.

Wave erosion has then eroded less resistant sand and clay at B.

Cliffs have been formed at C when a more resistant rock, chalk, has been reached.

Figure 3 Swanage Bay

In this photograph the headland of more resistant chalk can be seen in the distance (D) with its cliffs, and just out of shot, stacks and stumps.

In the foreground (E) is Swanage Bay, eroded from soft clay and sand, as has happened at Lulworth; there are no cliffs but a wide, sandy beach.

Check your understanding

Tested

Outline the difference between concordant and discordant coasts.

Waves can be split into two main groups:

1 **Destructive** or **plunging waves** – these break with a steep descent with little **swash** so **backwash** is strong and erodes material. If plunging waves are close together this can form a rip current that removes a great deal of sand, making the beach even steeper and perhaps creating a bar offshore.

2 **Constructive** or **spilling waves** – these spill up the beach (the swash) quite strongly so travel a long distance and much water soaks into the beach so the returning water (the backwash) is weaker. These waves tend to move sand and other material up the beach towards the land.

Waves and landforms

Revised

Figure 4 Contrasting wave types

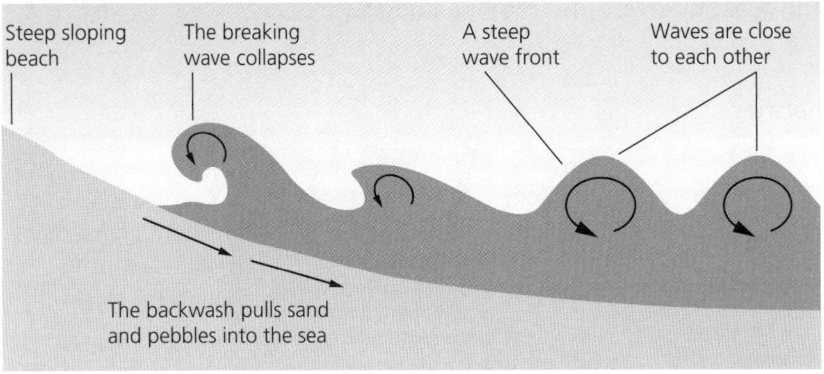

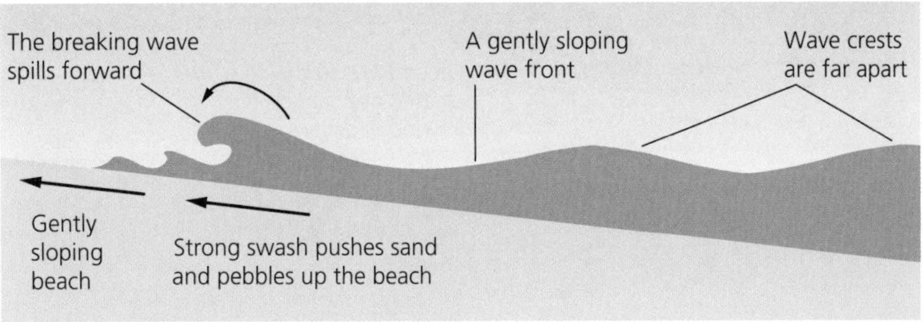

Knowing the basics

Check that you understand that constructive waves tend to add material to a beach whereas destructive waves remove material.

Check your understanding

Tested

Identify TWO differences between destructive and constructive waves.

Because waves usually approach a beach at an angle, they move material along the beach, as shown in Figure 5.

Figure 5 Longshore drift

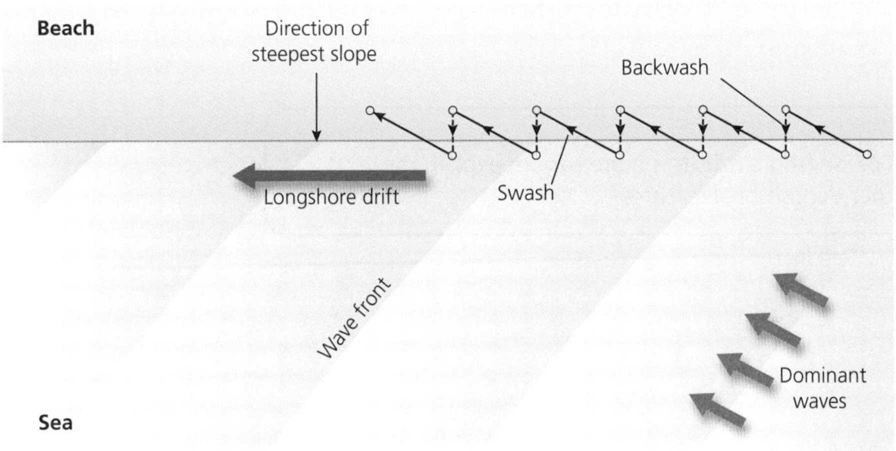

Stretch and challenge

Waves in deep water travel faster than in shallow water. So when waves enter a bay they tend to 'bend' – this process is known as **diffraction**.

1. The dominant wave carries material up the beach as the swash arrives at an angle.
2. However, the backwash returns with gravity in the direction of the steepest slope, taking particles of sand with it.
3. So material is moved along the beach in a series of swash/backwash movements known as **longshore drift**.

How longshore drift forms characteristic landforms

Revised

The best known depositional landform is the beach itself, made up of material eroded from cliffs, brought down to the coast by rivers and moved along the coast by longshore drift.

Figure 6 Formation of spits and salt marshes

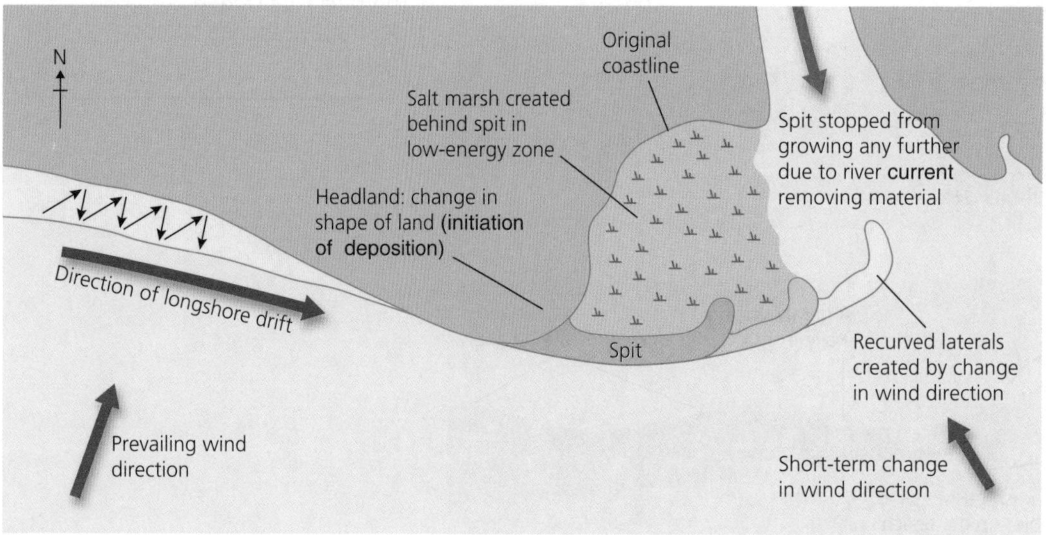

Another fairly common landform is the **spit**. As Figure 6 shows, this is formed as follows:

- Material is moved along the coast by longshore drift.
- If there is a change of direction in the coastline this material slowly builds up across the bay or river mouth.
- In the case of a bay it may eventually be closed off as the sand **bar** reaches the other side.
- In the case of a river it is likely that the deposition will end when the water becomes too deep and the current too strong.
- Sometimes spits have recurved ends if wind direction varies.
- Behind the spit in slack water **salt marshes** form.

exam tip

Once you understand the process of longshore drift it is quite easy to explain the formation of spits and bars and other depositional features.

Weathering, mass movement and sea-level rise

Revised

Weathering and **mass movement** are key processes in coastal erosion.

Weathering processes

- The most important type of **mechanical weathering** in the UK is frost weathering, where water enters cracks in the rock, freezes, expands and cracks apart material. Some rocks are porous and the water just soaks into them as it would a sponge. These rocks are especially prone to frost weathering.
- **Chemical weathering** takes place when water reacts with minerals in a rock, for example dissolving limestone – even resistant rocks such as granite will break down into clays eventually through the process known as hydrolysis.

Mass movement

- Although cliffs are nibbled away at by the sea, waves very rarely hit the cliff face from top to bottom.
- However, the cliffs are still affected by groundwater flowing from inland through the cliff face.
- In wet weather rocks that absorb water, such as clay, will become very weak and any harder rocks lying on top of them will slide and slump.
- Gravity will be enough to cause rockfall when rocks loosened by weathering become detached from the cliff face.

exam tip

Most students forget about mass movement and weathering altogether when explaining why cliffs retreat and only talk about waves.

Climate change

Many observers believe that erosion, weathering and mass movement will become more active with climate change. These are some of the possible reasons.

- Higher sea levels will increase the rate of erosion on cliff faces.
- Higher sea levels will cause flooding in low-lying coastal areas.
- Greater storminess will increase the power of waves and increase erosion.
- Higher rainfall will increase the risk of mass movement, especially slumping.
- Colder and longer winters will increase the amount of frost weathering.

Why does conflict occur on the coast, and how can this be managed?

Rapid coastal retreat – the causes

Revised

For this section you will have studied a section of coastline in some detail, focusing on the physical processes causing **coastal retreat** and the problems and threats that result from that erosion.

Some sections of the UK coast are retreating very rapidly indeed. One of the best known case studies is the Holderness coast in Yorkshire. This is outlined below but space is also provided for you to write in details of your own case study.

	Holderness	**Your case study**
Physical processes	• The coastline is 60 km long with cliffs of about 20 m • The dominant waves come from the northeast across the North Sea • Erosion takes place fastest when **tidal surges** combine with storms • Rates of erosion are the fastest in Europe at about 2 m per year • The rocks are mostly very weak boulder clay • The eroded material is carried out to sea so the beaches are narrow and don't act as much of a buffer • The rate of weathering and **mass movement** is very high because of high rainfall and winter frosts	
Problems and threats	• Good-quality farmland is being lost • For example, Sue Earle's farm was 150 m from the cliff edge 40 years ago • Today it has gone completely • Many villages have disappeared since Roman times – the land has retreated by over 4 km	

Knowing the basics

Erosion always causes loss of land. That land varies in value but in the UK that sort of loss is not insured.

Stretch and challenge

Coastal erosion takes place in fits and starts – for most of the time not much is happening although very weak clay is always being weathered and affected by mass movement.

How should coastal erosion be managed?

Revised

There are several choices about the management of coastal erosion. The most obvious choice is whether or not the cost of protecting the coast is worthwhile in terms of the savings made for individuals and the country as a whole. The management of sections of coasts in the UK is covered by Shoreline Management Plans.

	Holderness	Your case study
Conflicting views	The options are: **1** advance the coastline with **traditional (hard) engineering** **2** hold the line with hard engineering **3** strategic retreat **4** do nothing Those who want either option 1 or 2 include: **1** landowners **2** caravan park and holiday chalet owners Those who want either option 3 or 4 include: **1** the local authority **2** the national government	The options are: **1** advance the coastline with hard engineering **2** hold the line with hard engineering **3** strategic retreat **4** do nothing Those who want intervention: Those who don't want intervention:

Check your understanding

Tested

Describe the main purpose of Shoreline Management Plans.

Costs and benefits of traditional engineering techniques

Revised

There are costs and benefits of using traditional (hard) engineering techniques:

Sea walls	
Costs	**Benefits**
Expensive to build – as much as £10,000 a metre They aren't good to look at Access to the beach is restricted They can be undermined by large storms	Protection is generally good Land and buildings are protected Wave energy is reflected as the wall is curved
Groynes	
Costs	**Benefits**
Expensive to build – as much as £5000 a metre They need rebuilding every 10 years or so Trapping sand in one place means there is less sand elsewhere and so more erosion	Beaches are protected because groynes trap sediment/sand from longshore drift As a result cliffs are more protected
Revetments	
Costs	**Benefits**
Variable but can be as much as £1000 a metre Regular maintenance needed	Not unsightly Allow longshore drift to take place
Rip rap	
Costs	**Benefits**
Depends on sources of rock but can be £500 a metre Not always attractive and may obstruct access to shoreline	Absorbs wave energy Looks natural in the right setting
Offshore reefs	
Costs	**Benefits**
Moderate – about £600 a metre May cause hazard for navigation Upkeep costs	Create new intertidal habitat Visually intrusive at low tide

Anything done to change rates of erosion or deposition on one stretch of shoreline is bound to affect other stretches of coastline. For example, building groynes stops sand from moving along a shoreline with longshore drift so beaches beyond the groynes are deprived of sand and are more prone to erosion as a result.

That is one of main reasons why **integrated management** of coastlines has developed in recent years.

The costs and benefits of more modern approaches – moving towards sustainable management of coasts

Revised

Soft engineering

Soft engineering approaches involve less human intervention – a more 'natural' response to coastal erosion. They are not necessarily cheaper but they don't look as intrusive.

Beach replenishment	
Costs	**Benefits**
Highly variable costs depending on source of sand – might be pumped from close offshore or trucked in from distance Needs to be repeated every few years	Acts as shock absorber protecting structure behind the beach from erosion Totally natural looking Good for tourist business
Managed retreat	
Costs	**Benefits**
Retreat is gradual but people still demand compensation or insurance Some businesses are bound to be lost or damaged	Relatively cheap Natural processes allowed to happen which may slow down erosion – creation of marshes, for example
Cliff regrading	
Costs	**Benefits**
Depends on cliff but expensive to lower angle of cliffs Still requires other management techniques to prevent erosion at base	Prevents rapid retreat by slumping or rockfall Makes beaches and shorelines safer

Integrated coastal zone management

Integrated coastal zone management (ICZM) uses both hard and soft techniques as appropriate once areas are identified as belonging to one of the following categories:

1 areas identified as either needing protection or

2 best left unmanaged – a 'do nothing' approach.

The overriding aim of these policies is to be **sustainable**. In this context that means allowing/encouraging:

- economic development to improve the quality of life of people
- environmentally appropriate development that doesn't damage the natural environment
- equitable development that doesn't favour one group of people over others.

Knowing the basics

It isn't possible to prevent coastal erosion in the long term but you can slow it down.

Exam focus

1 Identify TWO reasons why some coasts erode faster than others. [2]

2 For a named hard-rock coast, describe its main coastal features. [4]

3 Which of the following best describes a discordant coast? [1]

A. Where the rocks run at right angles to the coast.

B. A down-market tourist area where many arguments take place on the beach.

C. A coast with many cliffs and wave-cut platforms.

D. A coast that is difficult to reach because of high cliffs.

4 Using Figure 3, describe the coastline shown. [3]

5 Outline ONE feature of destructive waves. [2]

6 Which of the following statements best describes constructive waves? [1]

A. They often occur during violent storms.

B. They add material to the beach.

C. They remove material from the beach.

D. The waves plunge vertically onto the beach.

7 Identify the process that moves material along a beach. [1]

8 Explain how spits are formed. [6]

9 Outline ONE weathering process that might take place on cliffs. [2]

10 Describe how mass movement causes cliffs to retreat. [4]

11 Identify ONE stretch of coastline where erosion is rapid. [1]

12 For a named stretch of coastline, explain why coastal erosion is rapid. [6]

13 Outline ONE feature of Shoreline Management Plans. [2]

14 What is the main feature of hold-the-line policies of coastal management? [2]

15 Name TWO methods of hard engineering. [2]

16 For a named coastline, explain how soft and hard engineering have been used in its management. [6]

Answers online

Online

Chapter 6 River Processes and Pressures

How do river systems develop?

Contrasts along a river's course

Revised

What rivers do:

1 They transport water and sediment from the land to 'base' level – this is usually the sea but might be a lake.

2 As a result they are the main mechanism for wearing away (eroding) the land.

There are huge variations between rivers and along one river's course. It is worth remembering that even the mighty Amazon, which discharges no less than 8 trillion gallons of water a day into the Atlantic, starts 'life' 4000 miles to the west in the high Andes, as a rocky stream that can be jumped across with ease. No one river has exactly the same characteristics as another but a few useful generalisations can be made about how rivers change as we move downstream from source to mouth.

Figure 1 The changing course of a river

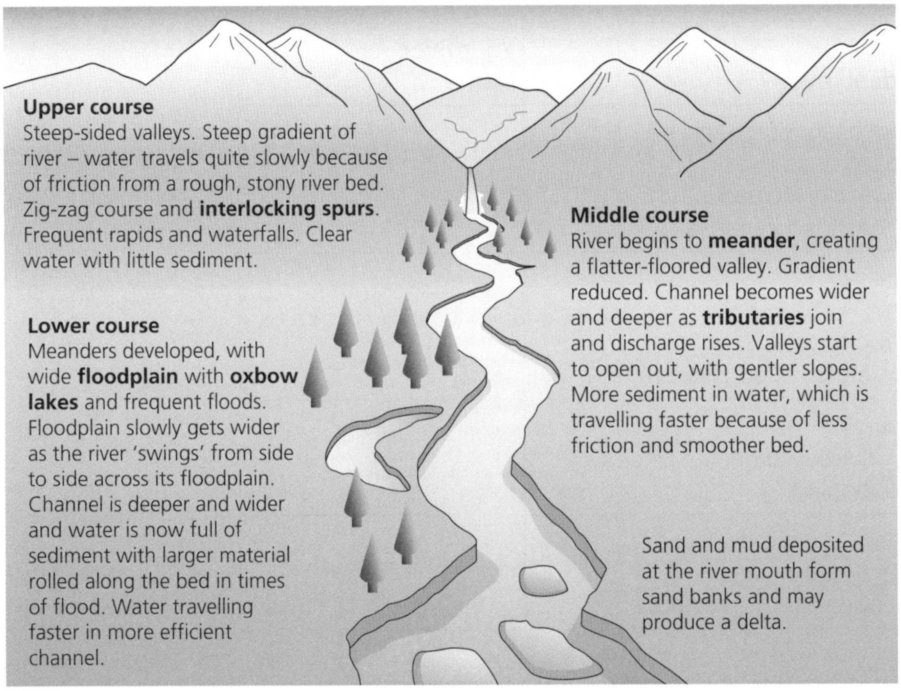

Upper course
Steep-sided valleys. Steep gradient of river – water travels quite slowly because of friction from a rough, stony river bed. Zig-zag course and **interlocking spurs**. Frequent rapids and waterfalls. Clear water with little sediment.
Middle course
River begins to **meander**, creating a flatter-floored valley. Gradient reduced. Channel becomes wider and deeper as **tributaries** join and discharge rises. Valleys start to open out, with gentler slopes. More sediment in water, which is travelling faster because of less friction and smoother bed.
Lower course
Meanders developed, with wide **floodplain** with **oxbow lakes** and frequent floods. Floodplain slowly gets wider as the river 'swings' from side to side across its floodplain. Channel is deeper and wider and water is now full of sediment with larger material rolled along the bed in times of flood. Water travelling faster in more efficient channel.
Sand and mud deposited at the river mouth form sand banks and may produce a delta.

Knowing the basics

In most rivers the width, depth and velocity of water flow all increase as you move downstream from source to mouth.

Changes in channel shape and characteristics

Revised

Figure 2 River long profiles – ideal and real (River Horner)

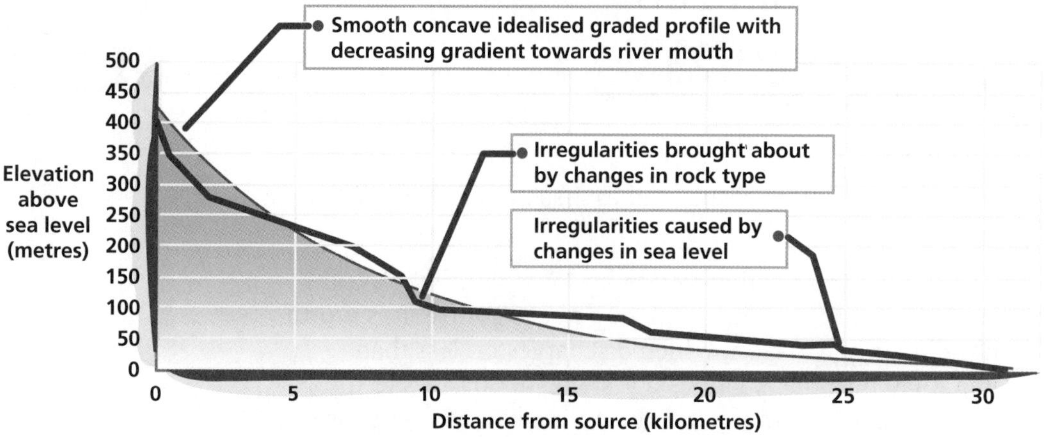

To revise this topic you need to have details of the **channel shape** and characteristics along a real river. As Figure 2 shows, the 'ideal' long profile is a generalisation; roughly true, but with obvious differences as well. Complete the table below with the key details for your river.

	The 'ideal' river	Your river Name:
Channel characteristics from source to mouth	Width of channel increases? River depth increases? Water velocity increases? **Sediment load** increases?	
Features of **upper course**	Waterfalls? Rapids? Stony/rocky bed? Narrow, steep-sided **river valley**?	
Features of **middle course**	Meanders? Wider valleys with gentler slopes? Small floodplain?	
Features of **lower course**	Meanders and oxbow lakes? Very gentle valley sides? Large floodplain with **levées**?	

Stretch and challenge

Models of rivers describe how they would develop in a 'perfect' world. In the real world rivers rarely have time to adjust to sea levels rising and falling.

exam tip

Most students imagine that valleys are formed by river erosion and nothing else. They ignore slope processes and weathering.

River landforms and processes

Revised

Processes

Rivers **erode** by:

- **hydraulic action** – the force of water striking the river bed and banks and often forcing air into cracks and crevices, so fracturing the rock
- **abrasion** – rocks and particles dragged by water across the bed and thrown against the banks will wear these surfaces away
- **attrition** – the rocks and particles themselves will be worn down and broken up
- **corrosion/solution** – water will dissolve rocks such as limestone.

Rivers transport their load by:

- **traction** – rocks and other particles are dragged along the river bed
- **suspension** – small particles are kept in the water itself until it stops moving
- **solution** – material is dissolved in water, e.g. salts or bicarbonates.

Check your understanding

Tested

Outline TWO processes of erosion.

Rivers deposit their load when they slow down as they enter a lake or the sea, or in sections of the river where friction slows down the water.

Typical lower-course features

Figure 3 Floodplains and levées

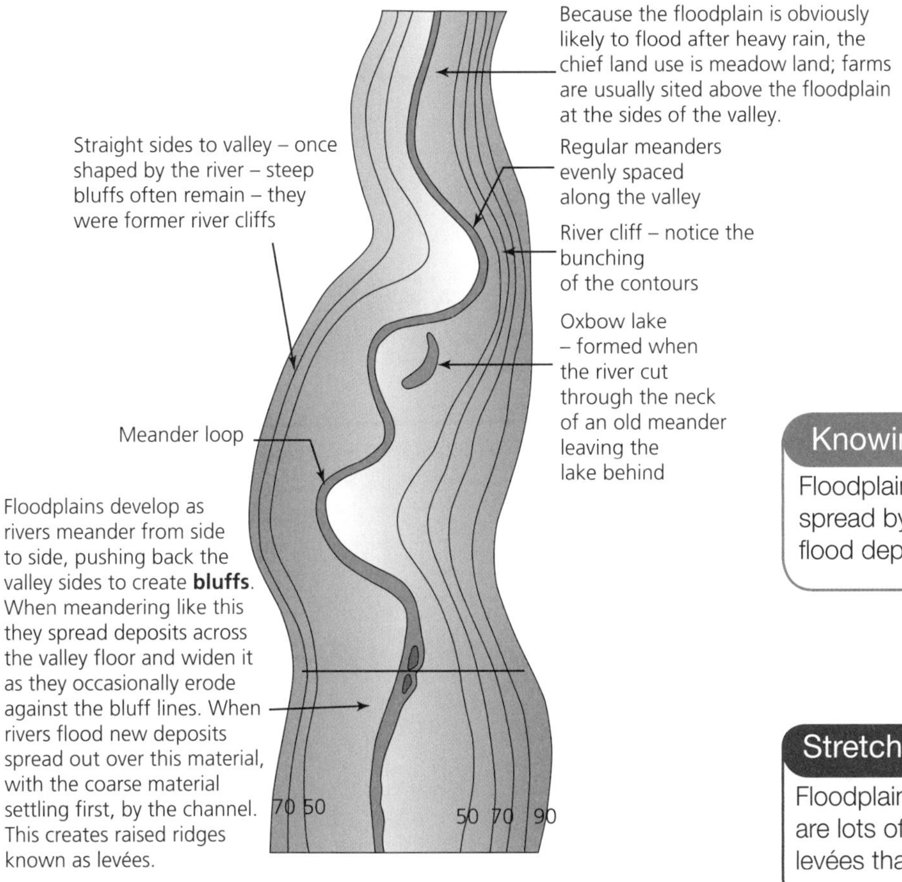

Because the floodplain is obviously likely to flood after heavy rain, the chief land use is meadow land; farms are usually sited above the floodplain at the sides of the valley.
Straight sides to valley – once shaped by the river – steep bluffs often remain – they were former river cliffs
Regular meanders evenly spaced along the valley
River cliff – notice the bunching of the contours
Oxbow lake – formed when the river cut through the neck of an old meander leaving the lake behind
Meander loop
Floodplains develop as rivers meander from side to side, pushing back the valley sides to create **bluffs**. When meandering like this they spread deposits across the valley floor and widen it as they occasionally erode against the bluff lines. When rivers flood new deposits spread out over this material, with the coarse material settling first, by the channel. This creates raised ridges known as levées.
70 50
50 70 90

Knowing the basics

Floodplains are made up of material spread by the river itself, covered with flood deposits.

Stretch and challenge

Floodplains are not really flat at all. There are lots of abandoned channels and old levées that make them far from flat.

Typical middle-course features

Figure 4 Meanders and oxbow lakes on the Blackfoot River

Meanders are formed when the faster-flowing water on the outside of the bend (A) erodes whilst on the inside of the bend (B), in the slower-flowing water, deposition takes place. In this way meanders become more obvious – inside bend deposition, outside bend erosion.

Oxbow lakes form when the neck of a meander (C) becomes so narrow that in times of flood the river simply follows gravity and cuts through it, leaving an old meander bend cut off. Deposition soon blocks up the old bend, creating a lake that slowly fills up with material over many centuries.

Figure 5 Meanders in close up

Water flows at different speeds in a channel – the water closest to a bank or a bed is slowed down by friction. Bends occur naturally so as water flows into a bend it keeps on going and, like a car going around a corner, the weight is thrown to the outside of the bend making erosion more likely there – the eroded material is then deposited in the slower-flowing areas further down the channel.

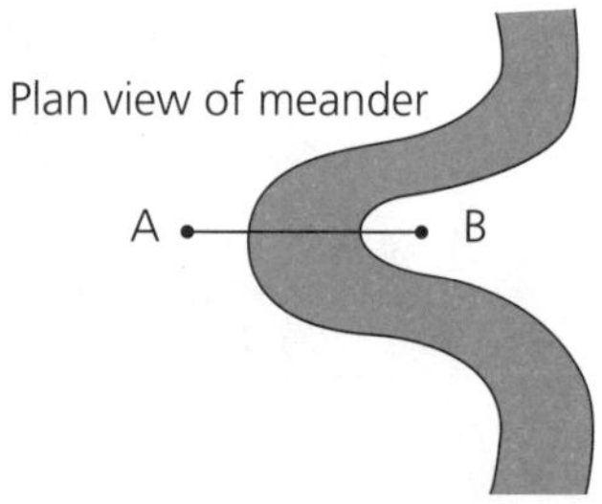

Cross-section of meander from A → B

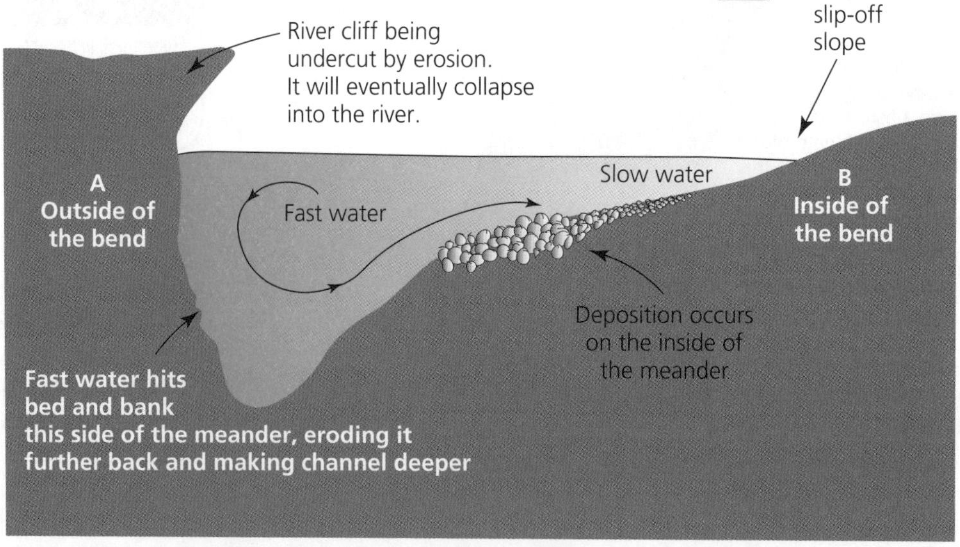

Typical upper-course landforms

Figure 6 The formation of a waterfall

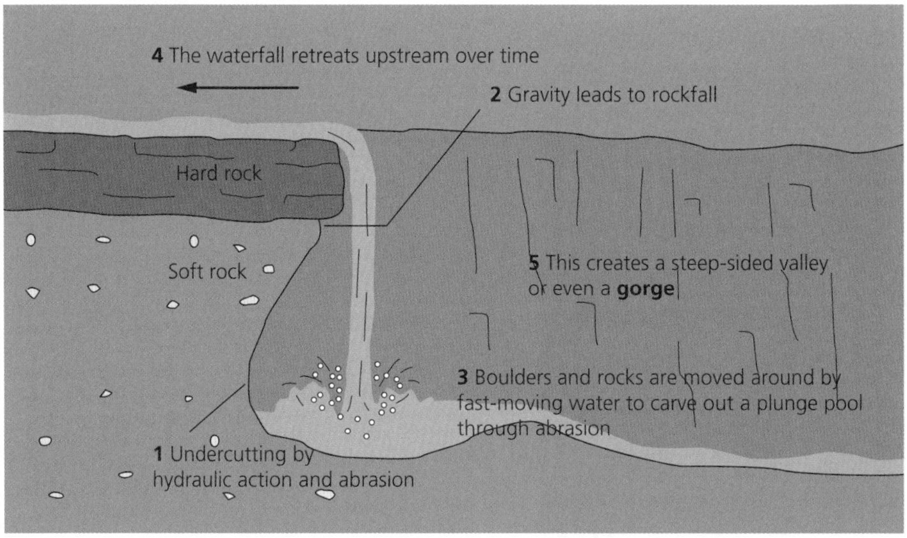

4 The waterfall retreats upstream over time
2 Gravity leads to rockfall
Hard rock
Soft rock
5 This creates a steep-sided valley or even a gorge
3 Boulders and rocks are moved around by fast-moving water to carve out a plunge pool through abrasion
1 Undercutting by hydraulic action and abrasion

Knowing the basics

Waterfalls retreat because, over time, erosion and weathering lead the waterfall face to move upstream as it is worn away.

Figure 7 Interlocking spurs and steep valley sides

Steep valley sides (A) are weathered by physical processes such as frost weathering which occurs when water enters cracks and crevices, then freezes and expands, shattering the rock. Mass movement such as rockfall and sliding takes this material down to the stream where it forms part of the **load**.

Streams cut down vertically. The bed is strewn with rocks and debris which are moved only very occasionally after storms (B). This material wears down the bed and the wandering course of the river creates interlocking spurs as the river cuts down. The river is not very efficient.

The influence of geology on slope processes

Revised

Figure 8 The Grand Canyon

The Grand Canyon is 450 km long and up to 30 km wide, and attains a depth of over a mile – about 1800 m. It is formed in an arid area so weathering of the valley sides is slow, especially on the more resistant rocks. The Colorado River and its tributaries cut their channels like a knife through butter through layer after layer of rock while the Colorado Plateau is uplifted; in other words, the butter is being pushed up into the knife too. Before the river was dammed the discharge would reach over 2500 **cumecs** in spring floods (the Thames only reaches 200 cumecs in exceptional flood conditions). This is enough to move very large boulders and cut into the channel bed further. This makes the valley sides steep and the canyon deep.

Valley shape

Gorges have near vertical sides because:

- there is little weathering or mass movement
- the river cuts downwards rapidly; perhaps the land is being lifted up too.

In different conditions the valley might be wide because:

- weathering and mass movement operate fast, as in a tropical climate
- rivers erode slowly.

Stretch and challenge

Rivers do most of their work in rapid bursts of activity when the water levels are high and the flow is rapid after storms or periods of heavy rain.

Sediment load

Rivers carry their load in three main ways – solution, suspension and **bedload** (or traction). Generally speaking, the amount of load increases from source to mouth.

How that load is made up differs according to the climate and the weathering and mass movement processes that dominate.

1. Rivers in tropical regions have high amounts of suspended sediment and look muddy. This is because chemical weathering is rapid, breaking down even hard rocks like granite into clay – the slope processes that dominate are sliding and slumping of material.
2. Rivers in Arctic and Polar regions have high amounts of bedload and little sediment in suspension. This is because physical weathering breaks down rocks into pieces, splintering them by frost weathering and the dominant slope process is often rockfall.

Knowing the basics

Remember that all rivers will have load carried in solution even in Arctic and Polar climates.

Why do rivers flood and how can flooding be managed?

Why do rivers flood?

Revised

Technically rivers flood when the amount of water in the channel exceeds channel capacity (**bankfull**) and they overflow like a bath with the taps left running! This happens naturally to all rivers from time to time, spreading material across a floodplain.

Figure 9 A storm hydrograph

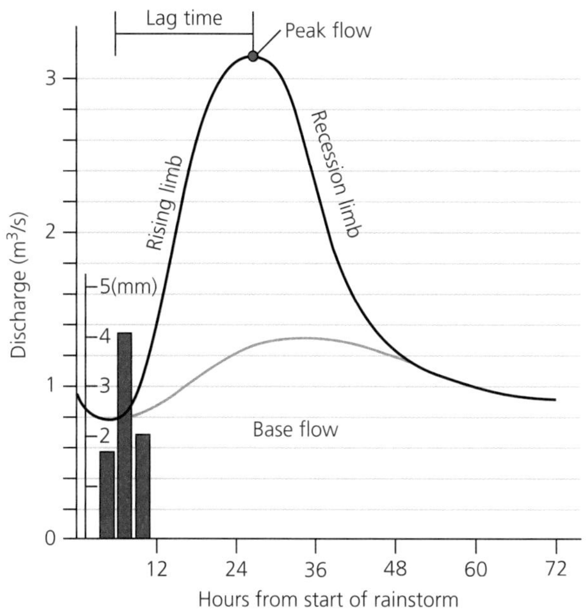

The **storm hydrograph** – a quick guide:

Time is on the *x*-axis starting when the rain event or storm begins.

On the *y*-axis we measure the amount of water flowing through the channel – its **discharge** measured in cumecs (m^3 per second).

The blue bar shows the amount of rainfall at different times measured by the inner scale (in mm).

In this example the river water begins to rise (and speed up) a few hours after the rainstorm begins – this is shown on the 'rising limb'.

Eventually, about 26 hours after the start of the storm, the river reaches 'peak flow'.

Once this water is passed downstream the discharge begins to fall and slow down – the 'recession (or falling) limb'.

If we assume that the amount of water that this river can hold (its channel capacity) is 3 cumecs, a flood will have occurred for about 12 hours on either side of the peak flow time.

Some rivers flood more often than others:

- Ground conditions – water either infiltrates into the ground and then moves slowly underground towards the river, or runs fast over the ground, causing flooding, including **flash flooding**.
- If the ground is hard or saturated already from previous rain, overland flow will take place.
- If the storm is violent and the rainfall very intense then rivers may not be able to cope.
- If a river is already near the bankfull stage from previous rainfall events then flooding is more likely. This is why rivers in the UK are more likely to flood in winter.

Stretch and challenge

Base flow is the amount of water in the river channel in normal conditions. This water reaches the river by moving underground as **throughflow**.

Check your understanding

Tested

Describe the main features of a hydrograph.

How people cause flooding

Revised

Figure 10 Impact of urbanisation on a hydrograph

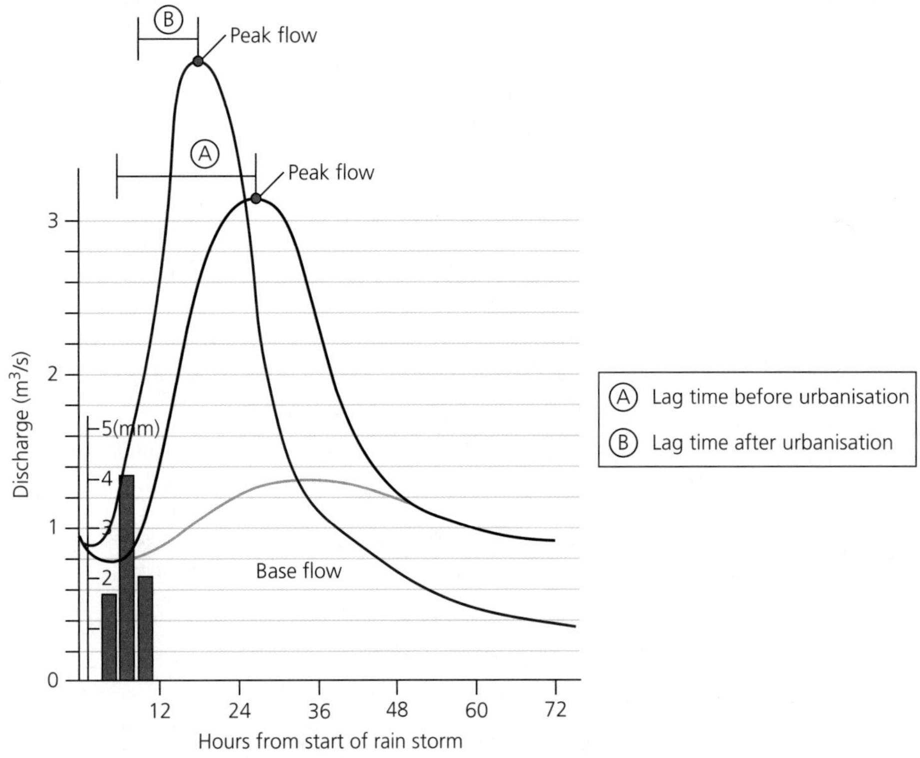

- **Urbanisation** increases the area of ground where water is going to reach the stream by overland flow because concrete and tarmac are not permeable.
- Drains below the ground will also deliver water quicker than normal soil conditions.
- If water reaches the river quicker then the peak discharge is going to be higher.
- As a result the river will flood more often.

There are other ways in which people interfere with what happens in river basins:

1. **Deforestation** – removing trees increases the amount of rain that reaches the ground (leaves intercept rainfall). Trees also use water to grow – removing trees reduces both evaporation and transpiration. So more water reaches the river, increasing flood risk.
2. Changing farm systems – replacing grassland with crops may increase **runoff**. Grass roots allow water to infiltrate even in heavy rain. Remove the grass and exposed soil can become waterlogged and overland flow takes place – this can erode the soil and cause river flooding.

Knowing the basics

Anything that makes ground less permeable (how easily it absorbs water) will lead to more risk of flooding.

Stretch and challenge

Remember that not all human interference increases flood risk. However, preventing a river from flooding in one place – say by building levées – will simply shift the water downstream so it may make the problem worse elsewhere!

Check your understanding

Tested

Urbanisation reduces **lag time** and increases **peak flow**. Explain what is meant by this.

Traditional flood defences

Revised

People have been defending their towns, cities and farmland for well over 2000 years. In the last few centuries these efforts have intensified and become easier with the invention of machinery to do the 'heavy lifting'.

For this topic you should have a case study that provides local details of the **flood defence** scheme and the methods used as well as the impact of flooding. Fill in the table below with your local details – of course, not all of the methods listed may have been used on your stretch of river.

Hard engineering method	Your case study
Embankments and levées These stop water from spreading into areas where flood damage could be costly. They can look natural and sometimes are built on top of naturally formed levées	**Embankments and levées?**
Channelisation Deepening and straightening a channel so it can carry more water. The bed and banks might also be reinforced with concrete to prevent erosion and shifting sediment – this can make navigation simpler on large rivers	**Channelisation?**
Dams Building dams is expensive but gives excellent flood control downstream. They are often ugly and intrusive but might bring other benefits such as better navigation and provision of power (**HEP**)	**Dams?**
Flood relief channels – pump stations Relief channels can be dug to divert water out of the channel in times of flood, and for smaller rivers pumping water into relief channels might speed up the removal of water	**Flood relief channels – pump stations?**
Wing dykes Building dykes out into channels at right angles to the flow traps sediment and also forces the channel to flow faster in the centre, which means it will erode its bed and become deeper. This increases the size of the channel	**Wing dykes?**
	The impact of flooding **1** **2** **3** **4** **5**

Soft engineering solutions

Revised

Hard engineering is frequently criticised not only on the grounds of expense but also because it isn't 'natural' – in many cases it just shifts the problem downstream.

Of course for cities on estuaries such as London, Amsterdam or Venice there isn't much choice but to employ hard engineering, but if soft engineering was employed upstream of these cities, flood risk might be reduced and less money spent on pouring concrete. On smaller rivers, soft engineering might offer more sustainable solutions.

As with the hard engineering methods, you should have your own case study details to use in completing the table below.

Soft engineering method	Your case study
Washlands/wetlands These are areas on a floodplain where flood water is allowed. Sometimes these are combined with levées and **embankments** but in this case they are set back at some distance from the river	**Washlands/wetlands?**
Afforestation Planting trees in the upper part of the river basin reduces the amount of water reaching the lower course	**Afforestation?**
Land use zoning In the past, low-lying land was rarely built on but pressure for development has changed that. Zoning allocates different uses to different spaces according to risk. Housing and commercial uses are kept away from high-risk areas which might be left as recreational space. Planning law enforces this	**Land use zoning?**
Flood warning systems The risk is accepted but better evacuation and warning systems are put in place. This allows people to evacuate and perhaps save some belongings as well	**Flood warning systems?**
	Others?

Knowing the basics

Most flood schemes use several different methods to protect people and property.

Stretch and challenge

Even soft engineering methods have costs – land not built on isn't profitable; forests may not be the most profitable use of land upstream. These indirect costs are rarely included in the calculations.

Exam focus

1 Identify TWO features of a typical upper course of a river. [2]

2 Which of the following best describes the lower course of a river? [1]

A. The water travels faster than in the upper and middle courses.

B. The channel is narrow and rocky.

C. The valley has many interlocking spurs.

D. The river is shallow and the bottom is clearly visible.

3 Using Figure 2, describe TWO differences between the idealised long profile and the real river profile. [4]

4 Outline ONE reason why a river long profile may not be the same as the idealised profile. [2]

5 Describe TWO processes which lead to a river eroding its bed and banks. [4]

6 Explain how waterfalls are formed. [6]

7 Describe the main characteristics of river floodplains. [4]

8 Explain how meanders are formed. [6]

9 Outline ONE reason why some valley sides are very steep. [2]

10 Describe TWO ways in which rivers carry their load. [4]

11 Which of the following best describes the point on the hydrograph when rivers are at maximum discharge? [1]

A. Lag time.

B. Rising limb.

C. Peak flow.

D. Base flow.

12 What is base flow? [2]

13 Explain TWO ways in which human action can affect a hydrograph. [4]

14 For a named river, explain how hard engineering has been used to reduce flood risk. [6]

15 Outline TWO soft engineering methods used to manage rivers. [4]

16 State ONE advantage of soft engineering. [2]

Answers online Online ☐

Section C Large-scale Dynamic Planet

Chapter 7 Oceans on the Edge

How and why are ecosystems threatened with destruction?

A marine ecosystem in detail

Revised

For this section you have studied ONE **marine ecosystem**, looked at its characteristics and then the problems that it faces. On this page and the next you will find the topic of **coral reefs** presented in the way that you will need to know for the examination – if you have studied a different ecosystem then fill in details in the boxes provided.

Figure 1 Coral reefs classified by threat from local activities

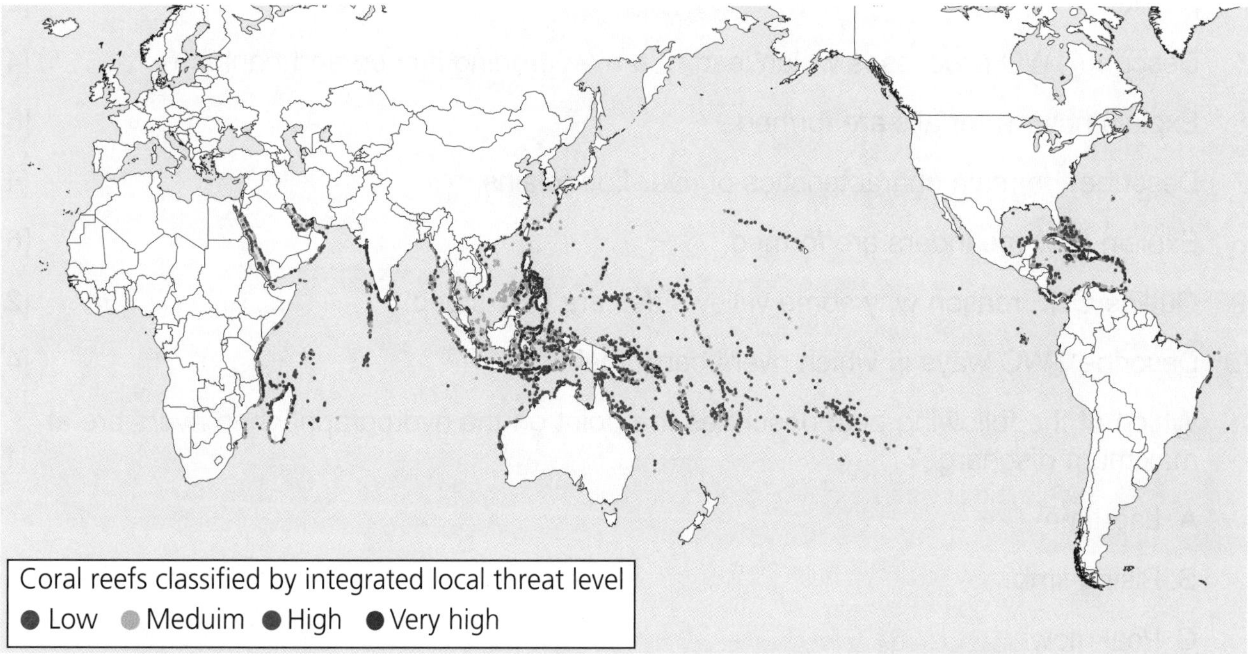

- Coral is a living organism that needs light to grow – once thought to be plants, they are in fact animals.
- Coral reefs are largely found in tropical waters where the temperatures are between 24°C and 26°C.
- They are found close to the shore both of the mainland and islands, usually just a few hundred metres out to sea.
- They provide a home for well over 4000 species of fish, which is over a quarter of all known species.
- They provide protection to coastlines from erosion.
- They are a major attraction for tourists.
- They provide aquatic fish for the aquarium trade.

Your chosen marine ecosystem	
Global distribution	
Characteristics (what is it like?)	
Human uses	**1** **2** **3**

A marine ecosystem at risk

Revised

Every marine ecosystem is threatened because of:

- global temperature changes leading to **sea-level rise**
- global temperature rise leading to warmer oceans
- the acidification of oceans as CO_2 levels rise
- the reduction of oxygen as nitrates run off the land in coastal areas
- pollution from shipping and the dumping of waste
- more sediment from the land reducing photosynthesis
- overfishing changing **food webs**.

As for the previous section you have studied a marine ecosystem in terms of the threats. The table below shows these threats in the context of coral reefs. If you have studied something different, complete a table like this for your marine ecosystem.

Threats to coral reefs
Global warming Warmer oceans lead to the **bleaching** of coral when the algae that live within it are unable to survive; this upsets the feeding cycle of coral. Local warming can take place following events such as **El Niño**
Fishing Some fishing methods are just plain destructive, such as using explosives (blast fishing). Fishing for aquarium species is also likely to upset the food web unless very carefully controlled. Many tropical areas are extremely poor and fish form an important part of the diet – with population increase this is likely to be a major pressure
Coastal development Coastal development almost always leads to an increase in sediment in rivers – disturbed ground, erosion of loose soil and the washing off of pollutants all have negative impacts on reefs that thrive in clear water. In some areas reefs provide **lime** for farming – such materials are in very short supply on many tropical islands
Tourism For many developing countries **tourism** is a major income source. Tourists are attracted by reefs but not all of their activities are positive. Not only do activities such as water skiing, scuba diving and surfing cause disturbance, but tourist resorts involve coastal development and increase the pollutants in **lagoons** – what exactly happens to the sewage?

exam tip

Try to avoid extreme statements in your answers. There are many threats to marine ecosystems but some are worse than others.

How marine food webs are disturbed

Revised

Figure 2 A marine food web

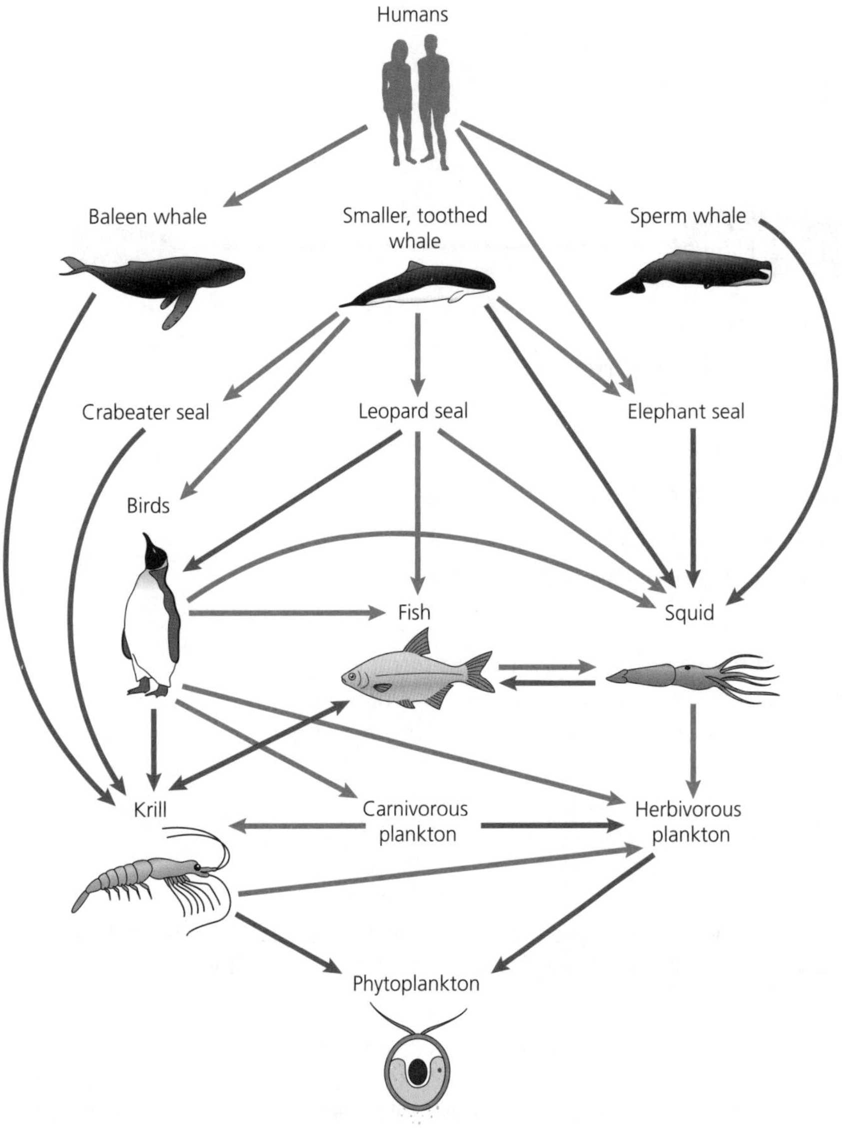

Disrupting food webs

Food webs are complex so quite small changes in one element can have large impacts on another.

Large carnivores are generally rare and quickly affected by changes in other parts of the web.

Examples:

1. Whales are still hunted and until recently most whale populations were falling fast.
2. Overfishing can affect both the population of fish themselves and the animals dependent upon them.
3. **Krill** are the cornerstone of this system. No one knows how many krill there are – maybe 500 million tons. And no one really knows the exact numbers of whales, seals and penguins that rely on krill or how climate change will affect those populations or krill numbers.
4. Krill are attracting the attention of commercial fishing for their protein value.
5. Krill live off **phytoplankton**. Unfortunately the global population of phytoplankton has fallen about 40 per cent since 1950. Global warming is usually identified as the main cause.
6. Worryingly, phytoplankton and other aquatic plants and algae consume CO_2 to produce half the world's oxygen output – equalling that of trees and plants on land.

Stretch and challenge

Loss of phytoplankton because of global warming is an example of **positive feedback** – oceans get warmer, less phytoplankton grows, so less CO_2 is consumed, so the atmosphere gets warmer, so the oceans get warmer.

Fundamental causes

The main causes of food web disruption are:

- overfishing
- habitat destruction
- pollution.

Eutrophication

The process of **eutrophication** is commonly associated with freshwater environments but it is increasingly a feature of marine environments too.

Nutrient cycling is critical to all ecosystems. However, when the flow of nutrients into the environment exceeds the ability of natural systems to absorb them, ecosystems feel the impact. The main cause of this excess is fertilisers used on the land and the results are often dramatic:

- Too many nutrients in marine systems can cause excessive growth of algae.
- This blocks sunlight and as it decays removes oxygen from the water.
- This reduces the diversity of species which cannot cope with reduced oxygen.
- This damages coral reefs and other marine ecosystems.
- In extreme cases it creates oxygen-depleted **hypoxic** or 'dead' zones.

Knowing the basics

Most densely populated regions have marine ecosystems that are either eutrophic or, worse, hypoxic.

Siltation

Coastal development frequently involves clearance of land for access to the coast. In many parts of the world tourist development has had unforeseen negative impacts.

Figure 3 Siltation

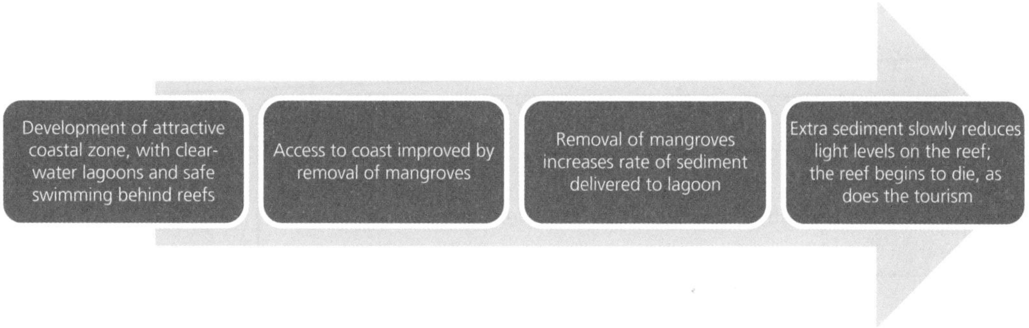

Development of attractive coastal zone, with clear-water lagoons and safe swimming behind reefs
Access to coast improved by removal of mangroves
Removal of mangroves increases rate of sediment delivered to lagoon
Extra sediment slowly reduces light levels on the reef; the reef begins to die, as does the tourism

The contribution of climate change

Revised

Without climate change the oceans would be in trouble because of waste discharge but climate change is clearly making matters even worse. For example, a study from Bristol University claims that acidification is progressing faster than at any time during the past 65 million years, with potentially devastating effects for marine ecosystems.

Acidification

The oceans are getting more acidic because of increased CO_2 in the atmosphere. Between 1751 and 1994 surface ocean **pH** is estimated to have decreased from approximately 8.25 to 8.14; this is an increase of 30 per cent in acidity. About a quarter of the CO_2 in the atmosphere is taken up by the sea so the more CO_2 there is in the atmosphere, the more acidic oceans become.

Warming

Warmer water is less able to absorb the extra CO_2 being pumped into the atmosphere as a result of burning fossil fuels, and as seawater warms it also expands, causing a rise in sea levels. Both will have an impact on the health of the oceans and, of course, global temperatures.

Stretch and challenge

The warming of the oceans is an excellent example of positive feedback. The oceans are warming up because of more CO_2 in the atmosphere but because the oceans can absorb less CO_2 as they warm up, there is more left in the atmosphere, making the oceans warmer and so on.

Bleaching

Sea temperatures in the tropics have increased by almost 1 °C over the past 100 years and are currently increasing at the rate of approximately 1–2 °C per century. Reef-building corals, which are central to healthy coral reefs, are currently living close to their upper thermal limit.

Sea-level rise

Sea levels rose by 1.5 mm per year in the period from 1961–2003. This happens because of melting ice and the expansion effect of warming up water. This can have a devastating effect on marine ecosystems as light has further to travel in deeper water, quite apart from flood risk and the threat of introducing salty water into previously freshwater environments.

exam tip

Make sure that you don't muddle up questions that ask you 'why' something has happened and the 'results' of a process. Lots of students know quite a bit about the causes of climate change and sometimes want to show it off, even when the question is about results and not causes.

Investigating the local pressures on a named ecosystem

Revised

Marine ecosystems support local populations. In many cases those populations are growing – that is a pressure in itself and the demands they are making are also growing. You will have studied ONE ecosystem to illustrate these pressures. The table below has been completed with respect to coral reefs but if you studied a different ecosystem then fill in the details in the spaces provided.

	Chosen ecosystem: coral reefs **Chosen location: St Lucia**	**Your chosen ecosystem:** **Your chosen location:**
Pressure 1	**Tourism** Tourism is the main industry on the island (45% of GDP) and the reefs are important – tourists wish to enjoy water sports, go snorkelling, dive and fish. Unmanaged, all of these will disturb the reef but the income is important and generates jobs	
Pressure 2	**Growing population and runoff waste** As the population grows and as tourist resorts grow there is a growing problem of coastal development. This creates waste which may run off into the lagoon and eventually the reef, where damage is likely. The population grew from 130,000 in 1990 to 170,000 in 2010	
Pressure 3	**Fishing** St Lucia is very poor and fish are an important part of the diet. Most fishermen do not have the equipment to fish in deep water so with a growing population overfishing on reefs is very likely to be upsetting the food web. An example of these problems is in Soufrière Bay	

How different local groups may disagree about management

Revised

As before the content here depends upon your chosen case study. The example used once again is coral reefs but many of the groups may apply to your own chosen ecosystem if different. In each case the conflicts are usually the result of:

- economic gain for one group meaning a loss for another group
- many different groups depending on the ecosystem and each believing that it should have priority over the others
- the temptation to take short-term benefits (usually income) now rather than worry too much about the long-term costs.

Group 1: **Local fishermen** have used the reefs as a source of food for centuries. Growing demand for food, some of it to satisfy local tourist demand, threatens the ecosystem by taking key species from the food web, sometimes with damaging methods such as using poison. In some cases fishermen are also involved in a profitable trade for aquarium species.

Group 2: **Tourists** enjoy snorkelling and diving and other water sports – these disturb the fish population, thus coming into conflict with local fishermen. There may be conflicts within different groups – snorkellers and water skiers for example!

Group 3: **Private yachts and cruise ships** inevitably produce disturbance, not least from their propellers and the waste they generate. The former physically damage reef species while the latter produces chemical changes in the water which can upset the food web and lead to eutrophication. Oil discharged from large cruise liners is especially damaging.

Group 4: **Local farmers** trying to improve their lives may be using fertilisers such as nitrates. These enter the groundwater and eventually the lagoon thus increasing eutrophication and posing a risk for the whole reef.

Group 5: **Local businesses** often depend on tourism. Shopkeepers, bar owners and hoteliers are frequently aware that many tourist activities threaten the reef's long-term survival but their concern is often short-term 'survival'.

Stretch and challenge

There is frequently a 'geography of profit' involved here. The groups that benefit – shareholders for large resort companies – may not live in the areas that are being developed and changed.

Local case studies of marine management

Revised

You will have studied two case studies of local marine management. The goal of many of these **management schemes** is to:

- allow local enterprises to continue to operate
- ensure that the marine ecosystem in not threatened by these activities and conflicts.

The table below has been completed for the St Lucia case study of marine management in Soufrière and a column left blank for you to complete notes for your second case study.

Case Study 1: Soufrière (St Lucia)	Case Study 2:
Fact file Management of coral reefs St Lucia – Caribbean island Much local poverty Increasing dependency on tourist income	**Fact file**
Problem Multiple activities have caused visible problems for the reefs and a threat to their survival – see page 68	**Problem**
Plan To create different zones on the reefs permitting different activities in different places – this was the SMMA (Soufrière marine management area). This was formed in 1992 and reviewed/updated in 1997. Locals were trained to police the area using funds from tourist taxes to make this self-financing	**Plan**
Remaining issues The dependency on tourism is increasing and coastal development inevitably threatens the reefs. Mud washed down into the lagoons and onto the reef is very damaging and coastal development increases this risk	**Remaining issues**

Knowing the basics

Remember that there will always be arguments about using a resource like a reef. Sustainable management involves helping people agree that cooperation is the best route forward.

Global solutions to the declining health of the oceans

Revised

In the end small-scale or even larger, regional-scale efforts to tackle the problems of the oceans are doomed to failure unless the longer-term international issues are dealt with. The causes of the many problems go way beyond the control of an individual government, even a powerful superpower such as the USA.

- Forty per cent of the oceans are controlled by nation states. This includes a 12-mile zone offshore which is owned by the country and a 200-mile zone where countries have economic rights over the ocean. That leaves 60 per cent of open ocean as 'the common heritage of mankind' controlled by the International Seabed Authority.
- Recent history is not encouraging. One expert commented that 'Less than one per cent of global ocean surface is effectively protected nowadays' (Ricardo Aguilar, Research Director for Oceana Europe).

Since the 1980s there has been increasing concern not just about the chemistry and temperature of seawater but also the growth of 'garbage patches'. The best known of these is the 'Great Pacific Garbage Patch'. Eighty per cent of this garbage is thought to come from land-based sources and 20 per cent from ships. A typical 3000-passenger cruise ship produces over eight tonnes of solid waste weekly, much of which ends up in the patch.

- Marine Protected Areas offer a route forward; there are an estimated 2679 globally.
- However, many present MPAs exist only as 'paper parks'; laws are not enforced and resources not available.
- In many other MPAs pressures outside parks and reserves undermine the local policies.
- Of 1147 sites assessed for their effectiveness at reducing the threat of overfishing, 15 were rated as effective, 38 were partially effective and 47 were rated not effective.

Figure 4 Marine Protected Areas classified according to management effectiveness rating

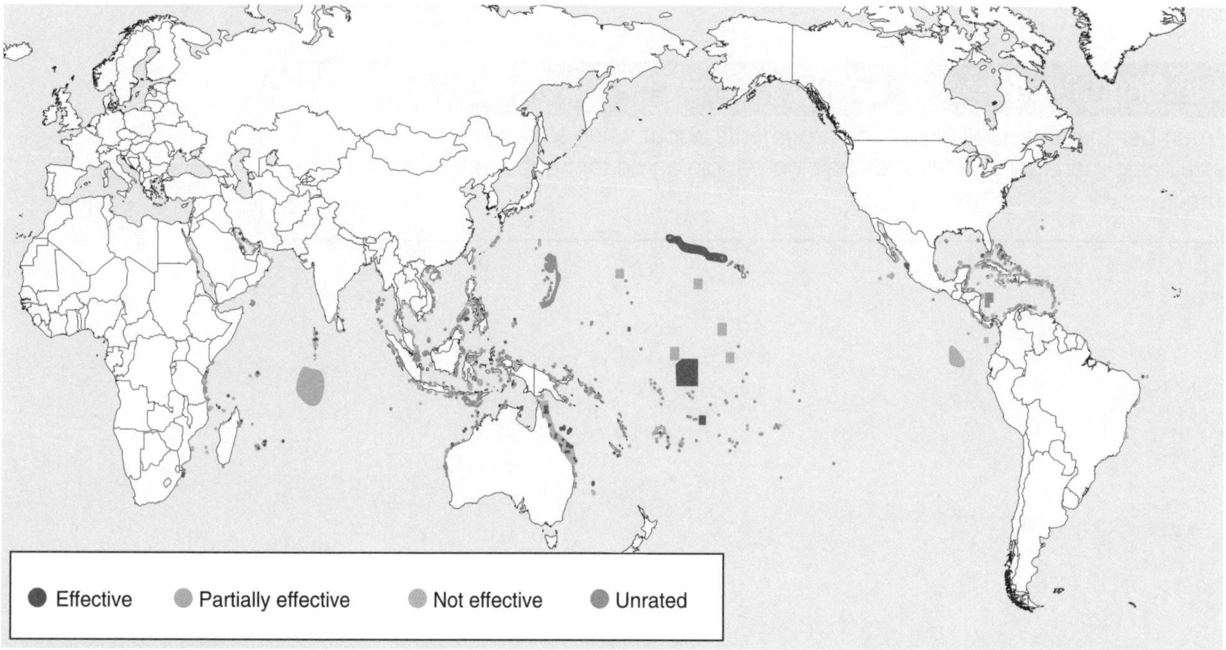

Exam focus

1 Using Figure 1, describe the global distribution of reefs at risk. [3]

2 Which of the following is an accurate statement about coral reef distribution? [1]

A. There are more reefs in the Indian Ocean than in any other ocean.

B. There are more reefs in the Atlantic Ocean than in the Indian Ocean.

C. The largest number of reefs is in the Pacific Ocean.

D. There are more reefs in the northern hemisphere than the southern hemisphere.

3 Identify TWO threats to marine ecosystems. [2]

4 For a named marine ecosystem, explain why it is under threat. [6]

5 Define the term 'food web'. [2]

6 Outline TWO ways food webs can be disrupted by human action. [4]

7 Define the term 'eutrophication'. [2]

8 Outline ONE process that threatens marine life. [2]

9 Explain how climate change threatens the health of marine ecosystems. [6]

10 Identify TWO reasons why sea levels are rising. [2]

11 For a named local marine ecosystem, explain why it is under pressure. [6]

12 Outline ONE possible consequence for marine ecosystems of population increase in coastal regions. [2]

13 Outline TWO reasons why there may be conflict over the use of marine ecosystems. [4]

14 For a marine conservation scheme that you have studied, outline TWO ways in which the ecosystem has been managed. [4]

15 Identify TWO ways in which the oceans are controlled globally. [2]

16 Explain why the future of the oceans is so uncertain. [4]

Answers online Online

Chapter 8 Extreme Climates

What are the challenges of extreme climates?

The characteristics of extreme climates

Revised

If you chose to study Extreme Climates rather than Oceans on the Edge (Topic 7) you will have had to make a further choice about which Extreme Climate to study. This would have been either:

- a **polar region** such as Alaska or Siberia or
- a **hot arid region** such as the Sahel or, maybe central Australia.

In some sections, revision notes will be provided for both of these regions but on some of the other topics notes will be given for just ONE region with spaces for you to fill in the details of the other if relevant to your chosen climate.

	Polar	Hot arid
Temperatures	Long, cold winters, short summers – average monthly temperatures often below zero and in true polar regions never above 10 °C	Long, hot summers, little annual variation – average monthly temperatures frequently above 30 °C and never below 15 °C
Precipitation	Dry – often less than 300 mm per year; most precipitation is snow	Dry – often less than 500 mm per year; most precipitation is in the form of short but heavy, localised rainstorms
Other features	24 hours of daylight in summer, 24 hours of night in winter. Very short growing season. Often very windy	No 'winter' – sometimes a wetter and slightly cooler period. Clear skies, so nights can be cold

In truth, climates do not change abruptly from one region to another so these terms should be used with care.

In both cases the challenges to all living creatures are provided by the extreme temperatures made worse by other features such as the windiness or the lack of water.

Knowing the basics

Make sure that you know something about both temperature and precipitation for your chosen extreme climate.

exam tip

Questions might ask you to describe the climate – try to cover at least some detail in your answer and, if possible, use figures.

Adapting to the extremes

Revised

There are very few environments on Earth in which life cannot survive in some form or other. However, in order to survive, species have **evolved** methods of coping – **adaptations** that make their survival more likely. In this section we look at a few examples of these adaptations for the **fauna** (animals) and **flora** (plants) that live in hot arid climates.

	Hot arid	Polar
Adaptation 1 – Flora	Because of water shortages many plants have extensive root systems that both spread out over large areas and go as deep as 40–50 m into the ground to find water	
Adaptation 2 – Flora	Water is stored in the roots, stems, and/or leaves of plants. The plants that do this are called succulents	
Adaptation 3 – Fauna	Desert animals have adapted many ways to help them keep cool and use less water. Camels, for example, have large fatty deposits that store water (their humps). Many desert animals only come out to hunt at night when it is cooler	
Adaptation 4 – Fauna	Many desert animals are very small with a large surface area to lose heat, including features such as big ears	

Knowing the basics

Make sure that you know the difference between flora and fauna.

Stretch and challenge

Extreme climates pose challenges – there may be ways to adapt but there are fewer plant and animal species in these regions than in less difficult environments.

exam tip

Make sure that you read the question very carefully – it might ask you about plant adaptations or animal adaptations, or both.

How people adapt

Revised

Extreme climates have low **carrying capacities**. That is to say that they don't support large populations from their own resources. Obviously people can be kept healthy by importing the necessities for life from outside, so there are cities in the desert and in the Arctic, usually because of the presence of some vital resource (for example, gas in Siberia), but these communities do not live off the land. Like the Antarctic scientific research stations they are totally dependent on outside supplies.

If you have studied polar regions, complete a table like this for your chosen climate.

Coping with hot arid climates	
Food supplies and farming	Traditionally, **indigenous** people (the 'locals') in dry regions such as the Sahel save water by planting crops into carefully dug holes. These are known as Zai in the Sahel. As many as 25,000 Zai are dug during the dry season in each hectare! After digging the pits, composted organic matter is added and after the first rainfall, the matter is covered with a thin layer of soil and the seeds placed in the middle of the pit. In more modern times water has been provided by bore holes although many question whether this can be sustainable if arid areas get more arid in future.
Building design	Many traditional houses are built around a central courtyard to allow cross ventilation, and narrow streets help channel air to keep it moving. Window sizes are often small and shuttered to keep heat out. Modern adaptations include sinking houses below ground level and using solar panels to provide electricity for fans, again to keep air moving.
Body shapes and clothing	Human beings have also adapted – as with animals, certain human shapes are better adapted than others. Masai are tall and slender – an advantage in terms of losing body heat. The key to clothing design for hot climates is looseness to allow air circulation.
Transport and communications	In the past, travelling in hot regions relied on animals that can cope without water, such as camels. Much movement took place at night or at least before the heat of the day. In modern times it has become important to develop new types of concrete and surfacing for roads and runways, as well as dealing with expansion of rail lines.
Energy conservation and use	Living in hot climates is all about getting rid of excess heat. This is a particular problem in urban areas with their **heat island** effect. For existing cities the development of parks and irrigated green areas can help. In fact, the coolest regions in the Phoenix metropolitan area are those regions of **irrigated** agriculture or well-irrigated residential land use.

exam tip

Whichever your chosen climate remember that if you are asked, for example, to 'Outline ONE feature of building design' for two marks, you need to make one basic point and a development of that point for the second mark.

The cultural heritage of indigenous people

Revised

In this section you need to able to comment on a couple of aspects of the lifestyle of people in your chosen region. This will cover:

1 the unique identity of the indigenous people

2 their value in modern society.

In the next section you will look at the threats to people living in these regions but it is obvious that much has changed in the past few hundred years, especially in the past 50 years when many remote communities have been connected to the rest of the world. If you have chosen hot arid environments, then complete a table like this for your chosen region.

	Polar regions
Cultural uniqueness – point 1	Polar people have long had to live on what they could hunt. High-meat diets are inevitable. So whale and seal hunting are important and the ceremonies that surround these activities are part of what makes them what they are – their cultural identity. Most of the societies are tribal with no central leadership, often living in remote bands.
Cultural uniqueness – point 2	In common with many other hunting societies polar inhabitants such as the Inuit are frequently **nomadic**, moving as the food moves between winter and summer regions, living in different types of shelter: igloos in winter and portable tents made of animal hides and skins in summer.
Values – point 1	Inuit treat people, the land, animals and plants with equal respect. They try to use the resources wisely in order to preserve them for future generations. Strict hunting rules help maintain this balance, for example, by forbidding the killing of any animal in its mating season. Traditional knowledge of Inuit history, along with knowledge of the land, plants and wildlife, has been passed down through the generations. Traditionally, Inuit share the food they have hunted and everyone does his or her part to help those in need.
Values – point 2	Many Inuit communities continue to practise traditional song and dance such as throat singing and drum dancing. Oral history and storytelling are central to their **culture**, with tales passed down through the centuries. These stories are often about powerful spirits that inhabit the land and sea. They have been a continuing source of inspiration for Inuit artists – their clay sculptures and prints are well known to art collectors.

Knowing the basics

Remember that 'culture' is quite a broad term concerning the traditions and lifestyles of particular groups of people.

Stretch and challenge

Indigenous peoples were illiterate by our standards of reading and writing but they have always had a deeper understanding of the natural world because they live so close to it.

How can extreme environments be managed and protected from the threats they face?

The threats to people and natural systems

Revised

The threat to the lifestyles of indigenous peoples has increased very rapidly in the past 50 years. It was not so long ago that they were at best ignored by central governments; at worst they were excluded and persecuted. The threats today might be best summarised as:

- environmental problems
- social and cultural issues.

	Hot arid regions	Polar regions
Environmental problems	**Desertification** is the loss of farmland to desert. Soil is removed and whole regions become unproductive. Causes are many but include: • bad farming practices • overpopulation • climate change • uneven land distribution. It is often hard to identify which is the main cause and many groups explain the process in ways that reflect best on themselves.	**Permafrost** is very fragile and is threatened by both climate change and economic exploitation. A great deal of methane gas is locked up in the rotting vegetation that is currently frozen but would be released as it turned into marshy ground. Land is also being damaged by **resource exploitation**, such as the drilling for oil in Alaska or gas in Siberia which involves major networks of pipelines and much disruption of natural ecosystems.
Social and cultural issues	Most arid regions were either occupied by Europeans as settlers (Australia) or looted for their resources by **colonial** powers. Borders were drawn to create nation states that did not previously exist, dividing tribe from tribe, people from people. Cultural traditions were ignored or suppressed, local languages were repressed and replaced by English, French or Italian. Today cultural dilution is a consequence of: • the rising influence of western culture such as fast food, preferences for meat diets, styles of dress, use of alcohol • tourists' expectations to buy into a version of local culture as part of their experience.	Because polar societies were frequently very isolated they developed very distinctive cultures with groups separated by only a few miles. Until recently 20 languages were spoken in Alaska but increased contact between groups and government rules made: • English compulsory in the classroom • local names unfashionable, as they were officially discouraged. Changes to the economy of polar regions have undermined the subsistence lifestyle. Nomadism has declined, diets have changed and the old story-telling traditions have been eroded by modern media. Alcohol has often had a very damaging effect on local communities.

Stretch and challenge

Remember that it is widely thought that changes to the environment caused by global climate change will make these impacts more rapid and more pronounced.

The threat of climate change

Revised

In this section the threat of climate change is assessed. In extreme climates plants and animals are adapted to a narrow range of difficult conditions – quite small changes in the environment lead to large changes in the ecosystems.

Figure 1 The disappearance of Lake Chad

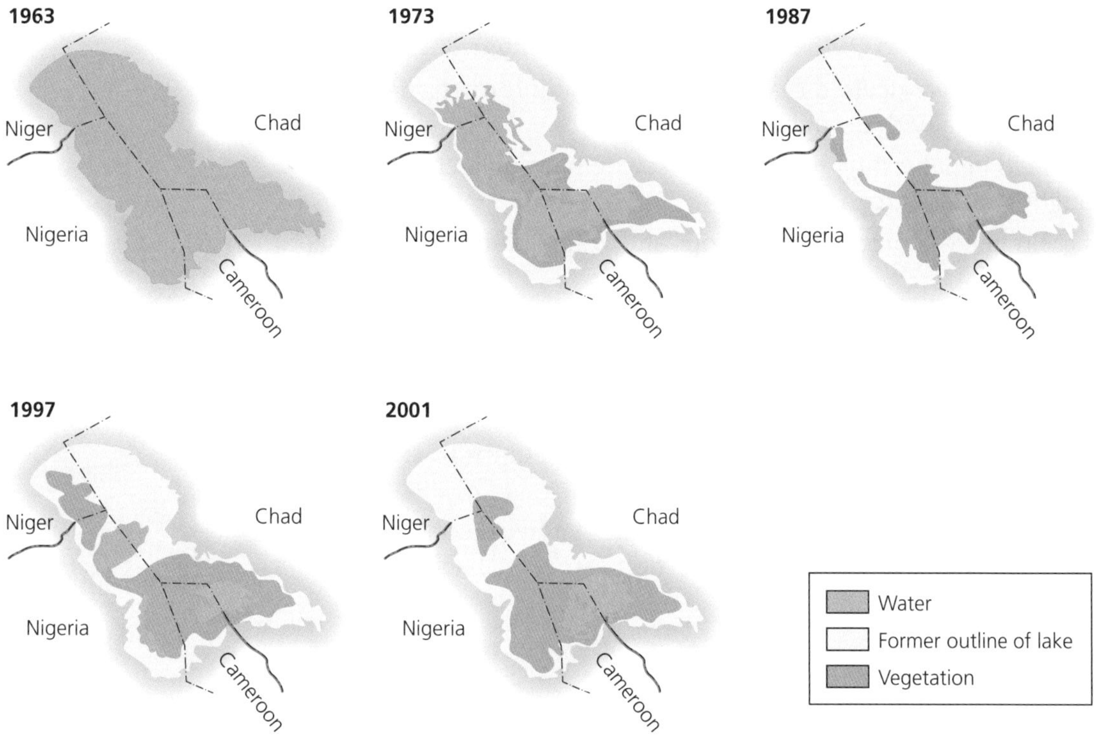

For hot arid regions changing rain patterns are the main result of climate change. Figure 1 shows the changing size of Lake Chad in the period 1963–2001.

To answer questions on climate change, remember the material that you revised for the previous topic and factor in the following:

Hot arid	**Environmental impact**	**Impact on people**
Changing rainfall	• Increased **desertification** • Soil erosion • Growth of sandy deserts	• Forced migration to find grazing land • Deforestation • Loss of cultural identity
Increased uncertainty and/or intensity	• More storms with more landslides/soil erosion • Drought elsewhere	• **Rural–urban migration** leaving stressed regions • Traditional lifestyles undermined
Polar	**Environmental impact**	**Impact on people**
Warmer summers	• Loss of sea ice • Melting permafrost	• Traditional lifestyles undermined • Migration to urban areas
Sea-level rise and warmer oceans	• Increased coastal erosion rates • Changing ecosystems	• Threat to local coastal communities • Loss of traditional food sources

How to adjust to changing climate

Revised

The role of local actions to cope with climate change frequently involves applying well-known and often traditional methods to mitigate the impact of a warmer climate.

Hot arid regions

- Coping with an unpredictable climate 'goes with the territory' in such regions.
- Farming methods that aim to conserve water are at a premium.
- Early warning systems are devised that provide relevant information to farmers to assist them in coping with drought.
- Farmers are trained in harvesting water, water-saving farming techniques and growing drought-resistant crops.
- The farmers are trained to produce their crops and wild fruit for commercial market.
- Intermediate technology includes:

1. use of **solar power** to provide electricity in poor rural areas
2. better water management to give better margins of survival as climate poses greater challenges – e.g. using cheap and easily repaired pumps to extract groundwater from greater depths
3. **conservation farming** – a form of multi-cropping that helps conserve water, increase crop yields and resist drought; production can be increased by up to ten times this way.

Polar regions

If you have studied polar regions, use this space to note three methods to help deal with climate change in polar areas:

Method 1

....

....

....

Method 2

....

....

....

Method 3

....

....

....

exam tip

If asked for 'methods' in a six-mark question it would be sensible to offer three different ways of coping with climate change with some local detail if possible.

The role of global actions in protecting extreme environments

Revised

Polar regions were amongst the first to attract the attention of scientists concerned with climate change. The popular imagination was caught with images concerning polar bears losing habitat and roaming into unfamiliar regions rather than the threat posed to indigenous people, but the message was clear. Things are changing!

Local actions can do a good deal to reduce the effects of, or even adjust to, climate change but in the end they cannot affect the timescale over which these changes take place. That needs global action. International efforts that have attempted to help include the following:

- The 1997 Kyoto summit tried to reach agreement on cutting greenhouse gas emissions – unfortunately the USA didn't sign the agreement and although China and India signed they weren't set targets for reducing emissions.
- The Copenhagen conference of 2008 failed to reach a binding agreement. The so-called Copenhagen accord 'recognises' the scientific case for limiting global temperature rises to no more than 2 °C but does not contain any promises to reduce emissions!
- The Antarctic Treaty (1961) limiting exploitation of the continent was followed by the 1998 protocol on Environmental Protection limiting economic exploitation of the continent.
- The Arctic Council was set up in 1996. This is an intergovernmental group made up of the eight Arctic nations (Canada, Denmark/Greenland/Faroe Islands, Finland, Iceland, Norway, Russia, Sweden and the USA) and six indigenous peoples organisations. The Arctic Council has only managed to put forward non-binding recommendations with no enforcement.

Figure 2 One of two Greenpeace ships on a mission to 'Save the Arctic'

If you have studied hot arid regions use the first TWO bullet points but add TWO more specific to your chosen climate.

Global action 1

....

....

Global action 2

....

....

Exam focus

1 For either polar or hot arid regions, describe TWO features of their climate. [4]

2 Which of the following is an accurate statement about your extreme climate? [1]

A. A climate with a great deal of variation.

B. A climate that is always stormy.

C. A climate that has little precipitation.

D. A climate in which it is impossible to live.

3 What is meant by 'species have adapted to the climate'? [3]

4 Outline TWO examples of how animals have adapted to your chosen climate. [4]

5 Briefly explain why extreme climate areas have low 'carrying capacities'. [2]

6 For your chosen extreme climate, explain how people have learned to cope with its challenges. [6]

7 Which of the following is the best definition of indigenous people? [1]

A. Newly arrived migrants to a region or country.

B. People who lived in a region or country before Europeans arrived.

C. People who have lived to a great age.

D. People who live in houses known as 'indigs'.

8 For your chosen extreme climate, describe TWO features of the culture of its people. [4]

9 For a named extreme climate region, describe the threats to its natural environment. [6]

10 Outline TWO threats to the culture of the people living in a region with an extreme climate. [4]

11 Using Figure 1, describe the changes in Lake Chad since 1963. [3]

12 Outline ONE way in which climate change might make a region of extreme climate more challenging. [2]

13 Identify TWO strategies that might be used to cope with climate change. [2]

14 Describe the role of intermediate technology in improving life in a region of extreme climate. [4]

15 For your chosen extreme climate, explain the global actions that have been taken to address the threats. [6]

16 Suggest TWO reasons why global agreement about protecting extreme climate areas is so difficult to reach. [4]

Answers online Online